A SHORT HISTORY OF DUBLIN

D0063850

First published in 2000 by Mercier Press
PO Box 5 5 French Church Street Cork
Tel: (021) 275040; Fax: (021) 274969
E-mail: books@mercier.ie
16 Hume Street Dublin 2
Tel: (01) 661 5299; Fax: (01) 661 8583
E-mail: books@marino.ie

Trade enquiries to CMD Distribution
55A Spruce Avenue
Stillorgan Industrial Park
Blackrock County Dublin
Tel: (01) 294 2560; Fax: (01) 294 2564
E.mail: cmd@columba.ie

© Pat Boran 2000

ISBN 1 85635 298 6

10 9 8 7 6 5 4 3 2 1
A CIP record for this title is available
from the British Library

Cover design by SPACE
Printed in Ireland by ColourBooks,
Baldoyle Industrial Estate, Dublin 13

A SHORT HISTORY OF DUBLIN

PAT BORAN

MERCIER PRESS

For my mother, Nancy Boran

CONTENTS

INTRODUCTION

Though it is generally agreed that the area around modern Dublin has seen human activity for the last seven to eight thousand years, there is some dispute about the precise age of the Liffey-side settlement itself. Certainly the founding of the city by the Vikings in AD 841 marks an important point in its history, but long before the Vikings arrived the area was the site of a number of settlements of considerable importance. Further confusion was caused by the Dublin millennium celebrations of 1988 which were based not on the date of the original Viking encampment but, unaccountably, on the date of the first imposition of taxes, by the Irish king Máel Sechnaill II almost 150 years later.

Quite apart from the fact that the anniversary of tax laws is itself a strange cause for celebration in any city's life, the chosen date was not even accurate. Because of an error in the chronology of the fifteenth-century *Annals of Ulster,* the imposition of the first taxes is recorded as taking place a year earlier than it occurred in reality – i.e. 988 rather than the actual 989. (The same annalists, it should be pointed out, when they later realised their mistake, simply omitted a year altogether and carried on regardless!) So, and perhaps not surprisingly, the history of Dublin is by times a confused and confusing one.

To get a real sense of the city's development and to follow its evolution to the point where it has become home to approximately one third of Ireland's entire population, it is necessary to take a brief trip back to the time when the city of Dublin was still only an occasional, perhaps even a seasonal settlement.

1

THE PREHISTORY OF DUBLIN, *c.* 5000 BC–AD 795

The oldest signs of habitation around the area of modern Dublin date from about 5000 BC when Mesolithic (or Middle Stone Age) peoples hunted and gathered in the locality. Because of its wide bay and natural harbours, and the fact that there were then half a dozen rivers and streams converging in the area, the relatively flat expanse of land between the hills of Howth to the north and the Dublin and Wicklow mountains to the south would have guaranteed early settlers protection from attack from farther inland and, of course, easy access to the sea. Though hunter-gatherer societies are not known for their long-term settlements, tough winters are likely to have persuaded them to retire to secure quarters until the return of spring. Out of this pattern the first regular if not continuous habitation of Dublin is likely to have developed.

It was not until the arrival of Neolithic (or New Stone Age) peoples, however, about a thousand years later (about 4000 BC), that any kind of sustained settlement seems to have begun. Equipped with stone weapons and the resultant confidence such 'technology' brings, these

Neolithic peoples quickly supplanted their Mesolithic predecessors and, by the time of the Bronze Age (about 2000 BC), the focus of the settlement seems to have moved down from the hills to the north and south and closer to what is now the centre of the city. When the Celts began to arrive about 300 BC, they too were quick to site themselves close to the Liffey, attracted by the possibility of being able to cross this main east-flowing river at low tide. In fact it was this same means of crossing that gave the city what is now its Irish name, *Baile Átha Cliath,* or The Town at the Ford of the Hurdles or wattles, a ford being a natural low stretch in a river where crossing is possible, the hurdles or wattles presumably referring to some kind of bridge-like structure made of interwoven pieces of wood. (The term 'wattle and daub', of course, refers to the technique of building walls by weaving together light twigs, sticks and other matter, and coating or daubing the resultant structure with mud as a sealant. If some kind of bridge-like structure was in place, it is also likely that huts of wattle and daub were also erected, though it would be some time before the first wall of any such material went up around the settlement. Archae-ological evidence suggests that the first perimeter was marked by earthen fortifications.) At the same time it should be remembered that settlements in the area were not exclusive to the banks of the Liffey. As their names imply, the villages of Rathmines, Rathfarnham and Rathgar grew up around the sites of Celtic *raths* or forts, as probably did Dublin itself, each settlement being separated from the others by tracts of countryside.

For just over the next thousand years, or until the arrival

of the Vikings in AD 795, Dublin remained in what has often been called 'native Irish' hands. (Later history will show, however, that this phrase is at best one of convenience, with almost every new group of settlers considering themselves Irish within a couple of generations.) Already most of the important roads traversing the country ended here, many of them close to where the River Poddle (now underground) meets the Liffey. This area, south of the Liffey and opposite what is now the Four Courts, seems to have been the location of the black pool or *dubh-linn* from which the name of the modern city derives.

Prior to the arrival of the Vikings, Dublin could have been little more than a village-sized clutch of dwellings, though it appears to have been well enough known to feature under the name Eblana (a corruption of *Dubh Linn*) on the maps of the second century cartographer Ptolemy of Alexandria. Though Ptolemy himself never came to Ireland, the fact that he could draw on earlier accounts of travellers from north Africa and the Mediterranean belies the popular notion of an ancient Ireland cut off from the rest of the known world.

2

EARLY CHRISTIAN DUBLIN

Apart from occasional conflicts between opposing Celtic chieftains or *ríthe* little of real importance is recorded of Dublin until the arrival of St Patrick – to Ireland, it is said, in 432 and to Dublin in 450. (Part of the reason for the lack of earlier records, of course, is that consistent efforts at record-keeping began only with the arrival of Christianity and the emphasis on the book.) On a mission of conversion, having been first brought here as a slave in his youth, Patrick certainly helped to put Ireland on the Christian map, his arrival leading to the foundation of a number of monasteries, around Dublin and inland, which in turn led to intensified communications between the country and the rest of Europe. Among the many legends concerning this father of the Irish church is his discovery in Dublin of three holy wells which continue to bear his name. Of the three, the most intriguing was close to the site of St Patrick's Cathedral, its exceptionally pure waters at one time believed by many to be the secret ingredient of Guinness's famous stout, brewed nearby.

Being one of the main ports on the east coast, in the early Christian period Dublin naturally saw its fair share of monastic traffic. In fact, so impressive was the work of Irish monks at home and abroad, that by the year 660, just over 200 years after Patrick's arrival, the first Bishop of Dublin was appointed by the Pope, though the size of the settlement in which St Wiro found himself could hardly have justified his presence, the inhabitants being in the mid-hundreds. It should be clear, therefore, that it was Dublin's geographical location rather than its size which had attracted the Pope's attention. Situated close to the mouth of the Liffey (much wider then than it is now, after centuries of land reclamation), the steadily growing settlement was in an ideal position to act as a trade centre between ships from England and the continent and the various monasteries thriving throughout the country.

3

VIKING DUBLIN, 795–1014

Somewhere around the year 177, or some two and a half centuries before St Patrick, two rival Irish kings, so the story goes, decided to divide the country between them. A line was drawn from Galway in the west to Dublin in the east, and everything above it was said to belong to Conn of the Hundred Battles, while everything below was the property of Mugha, the king who would give his name to the province of Munster. However, like many such political arrangements throughout Irish history, this one didn't last. And, again like many such arrangements, the crux would prove to be control of Dublin.

Whatever about such stories of feuds and wars for possession of the settlement by the Liffey, the real development of Dublin as we now know it did not begin until the arrival of the Vikings, or Norsemen and Ostmen of Scandinavia to be more accurate, in 795. Because popular histories have tended to exaggerate their exploits (particularly in relation to the looting and pillaging of monasteries), it might be useful to remember that between the seventh and tenth centuries the population of Scandinavia as a whole rose to unprecedented levels, creating local wars and famines, and giving rise to a desire if not a necessity for overseas exploration. Advances in ship-building techniques meant that voyages could now be made increasingly farther afield in search of better and easier living. The fact that the longships in which these Scandinavians travelled were flat-bottomed also made it possible for them to travel up quite shallow rivers, hence their ability to raid inland monasteries and other settlements up to then considered remote. Of the large group commonly known as Vikings, it is important to understand that the ones who came to and settled around Dublin were predominantly natives of Norway.

The first encounter with these fierce Norse came in 795 when a prosperous monastery on Lambay Island, off the north Dublin coast, was suddenly set upon, with disastrous results for the monks. Encouraged by their success, over the next fifty years or so the Norse made numerous assaults on the eastern seaboard of Ireland, while their Danish counterparts (and, in many cases, rivals) in general travelled farther inland. Both parties were attracted to monasteries and churches, these being for the most part undefended and often the only repositories of items of any real value. Interestingly, of more than 100 raids on monasteries recorded by Irish annalists up to the year 810, less than a quarter were attributed to Viking invaders. The real enemies of the increasingly wealthy religious settlements, it seems, were the Irish themselves.

This helps to explain why, as early as 841, the Norse could feel comfortable enough to risk establishing a permanent settlement in Dublin, or Dyflin as they called it. Had they really kept up the amount of looting and pillaging popularly attributed to them, they are unlikely to have sat around and waited for their avengers – or competitors – to arrive. With the attacking and looting of monasteries already established as relatively normal behaviour for local warriors, the Norse – their somewhat exotic looks and customs apart – would have fitted right in. (Their name in Gaelic – *Fionn Gaill*, literally 'fair strangers' – indicates that they stood out to some extent among the locals. Incidentally the name of the new north Dublin county of Fingal, created in 1994, derives from another group of Norse who settled the area from the 10th century, and means the 'territory of the strangers'.)

While at first the monasteries had been a source of undeniable attraction, now the Vikings – Norse and Danes – began to see for themselves the benefits of settling down and resuming the lives which war and famine had interrupted back home. Solidly placed on the mouth and south bank of the Liffey, intermingling with the small community already there, the Norse set about the stabilising of trade routes with the establishment of a protected *longport*. This consisted of a settlement (with a slave market), almost certainly walled, on the high ground between what is now Dublin Castle and Christ Church Cathedral. (The modern High Street, from Christ Church Place to Cornmarket, was the main thoroughfare of the Viking and subsequently of the medieval town, remaining so until the seventh century.) Though it has been elsewhere suggested that the site of this original settlement was closer to the present areas of Kilmainham and Islandbridge, Viking artefacts found there are more likely the remains of ninth- or tenth-century burial grounds beyond the walls. Certainly evidence of the existence of a large flat-topped mound or *thingmote*, off what is now Dame Street, suggests that this area was the centre of the settlement, the place where councils were called, bargains sealed and laws enacted. It is interesting to note, too, that the present pattern of narrow streets in this and other areas of the city is likely similar to the original curvilinear pattern, still evident in Fishamble Street, and many of the names of those early streets, today little more than lanes or back alleys, give an indication of the activities and trades carried out in them. Among the many to have survived are Crown Alley, Pudding, Marrowbone and, more colourfully, Cut Throat lanes.

Wherever exactly the first settlement was, and whether or not the new arrivals moved freely between settlements, the Dublin Norse would have realised the advantage of controlling access to the Liffey, and the erection of a *steine* or ceremonial standing stone (which stood until the late 1790s) near what is now Pearse Street Garda Station signalled their intention to stay.

A Secure Base

The establishment of a secure base did little to endear the Norse newcomers to the locals. Despite the story of Conn of the Hundred Battles and Mugha of Munster, there was as yet no concept of the island as a unified whole – and so, of course, no question of a conflict between the combined Irish clans and the Vikings. Nevertheless, seventh-century Dubliners were no less suspicious and resentful of the new arrivals than they might have been of a neighbouring chieftain who had strayed beyond his territories. With the Norse now holding one of the most important harbours on the east coast, attacks from Irish chieftains were quick to follow.

The first real assault on Viking Dublin came from the Irish king Máel Sechnaill in 845. When he failed to rout the recent arrivals, Máel made the best use he could of the now well-established rivalry between the Norse of Dublin and their fellow Vikings, enlisting the Danes on his side. In the event he managed only to expose himself dangerously when the Norse Olaf the White repelled the combined armies of Danes and Leinstermen from the much coveted *longport* and identified Máel Sechnaill as an enemy to watch over the coming years.

Not content with capitulation, and probably fearing that the Danes would now want to be compensated for their efforts on his behalf, over the next fifty years Máel tried again and again to take the city, until in 902 the combined forces of the men of Leinster and the men of Brega succeeded in driving out the Dublin Norse. Máel's celebrations, if such there were, proved to be short-lived, however, for fifteen years later the Norse not only returned under Sitric II but this time took Dublin with a determination that showed they would not again be so easily removed. However, determination was also one of the qualities of Donnchad Donn, the Irish king of the O'Neills (Uí Néill) who, faced with the same problem as Máel Sechnaill before him in 936 avoided a long and costly war by having the entire Norse settlement burned to the ground.

The Norse, however, were not ones for giving up.

Though their settlement had been completely destroyed, they must have seen sufficient promise in the locality of Dyflin not to let it go. With the arrival of Sitric's son Olaf Cuarán nine years later, the area of Dublin was once again in Norse hands. So safe did Olaf consider the rebuilt settlement, in fact, that he now began to use it as a base for attacks on the west coast of Britain. This security of tenure continued until 980 when the new High King, Máel Sechnaill II (whose name must have conjured up visions of his fierce ancestor) routed the Norse armies at the Battle of Tara, causing Olaf to flee for safety to the Scottish island of Iona.

But if Máel Sechnaill II managed to hold Dublin briefly that year and, having lost it, retake it in 989, it wasn't until he received the help of an ambitious Munster king in 1000 AD that he managed to retake and hold it, giving the Irish their first real foothold in the settlement which had already been in Norse hands for the best part of 150 years.

BRIAN BORU

In the year 1002, on Máel Sechnaill's death, Brian Boru (Brian Boruma), the Munster king who had come to his aid, himself became the new High King. That Brian was not part of the Uí Néill dynasty to which Máel and all of his predecessors belonged meant that his succession was not without its difficulties or its dissenting voices. With the kingdom of Ulster still resisting him (a resistance which would not be overcome for another four years), Brian made the wise move of allowing the Norse king,

Sitric Silkbeard, to remain as ruler of Dublin, giving him time to focus his attentions elsewhere. (Incidentally, in 997, Sitric had been the first person to produce coins on which the name Dublin, still written as Dyflin, appeared.) In accepting, Sitric presumably hoped to avoid the expense of time and energy which had previously been devoted to the defence of the settlement.

While Brian's attitude to the Norse seems to have been more enlightened than that of his predecessors, it should be remembered that his will did not represent the feelings of the Irish clans as a whole. The country was still divided into the provinces of Munster, Leinster, Ulster and Connacht which, under their respective kings, paid little more than lip service to the High King. If anything, each local king was constantly on the lookout for opportunities for territorial expansion, and wary of ambitious smaller chieftains who might want to take his place.

Being located in the middle of his own kingdom, therefore, the growing settlement at Dublin not surprisingly attracted the attentions of Máel Mórda, the then king of Leinster. Though in theory answerable to Brian, in 1014, like Máel Sechnaill before him, Máel Mórda decided to enlist the help of disgruntled Danes in a bid to take Dublin for himself. Using Sitric Silkbeard as his mediator, and promising even more autonomy than that which was enjoyed under Brian, Máel managed to gather what he considered a sufficient number of Norse warriors for the task. The venue for their battle was to be Clontarf.

Luckily for Sitric Silkbeard, a last-minute dispute with Máel Mórda lead to his refusal to take up arms in opposition to Brian. On Good Friday 23 April 1014 Máel

Mórda and his allies from the Orkneys and the Isle of Man marched straight into utter defeat at the hands of the combined armies of the High King and a friendly Viking regiment from Northumbria. Though Brian Boru himself was killed in his tent after the battle (according to local tradition the tent was pitched in what is now Mountjoy Square, then the most southerly part of Clontarf) effectively the years of Viking dominance in Ireland were done.

This is not to suggest that the Vikings were driven out of Ireland after Clontarf. Though Sitric Silkbeard might have been instrumental in securing the services of armies hostile to Brian, even he managed to stay on, serving as king of Dublin under Brian's watchful eye.

This almost miraculous truce between Brian's successor as High King, Máel Sechnaill, and the Norse of Dublin resulted in the continued expansion of the city. In 1028, following a visit to Rome, Sitric assisted Bishop Donat in the founding of Christ Church Cathedral. A gift of farmland nearby, also made by Sitric, would enable the cathedral to support itself through the next 800 years. With a secure bridge now in place over the Liffey, at the site of the original ford, the avowedly Christian settlement was thriving.

LOCAL RIVALRIES

In the 150 years or so after the defeat of Máel Mórda, it gradually became clear to the Irish kings of Munster, Leinster, Ulster and Connaught that control of Dublin lead to influence in the church based there, and very likely influence in the matter of succession to the high kingship itself. Over this period, therefore, control of Dublin for the most part passed between lackeys imposed by the kings of the four provinces and their successors. With the founding of All Hallows, on the site now occupied by Trinity College, the focus of the settlement moved ever closer to the coast. However, it was the appearance of St Michan's Church 'without the walls' on present-day Church Street, and of the Cistercian St Mary's Abbey (once among the largest religious foundations in the country), off present-day Capel Street, that marked the first real expansion of the settlement northwards across the Liffey. (Interestingly it was to St Michan's that Bishop Samuel, as the self-proclaimed Metropolitan of Oxmans-town, in 1097 removed the ecclesiastical seat from Christ Church, perhaps thereby starting the rivalry between the north and south sides of the city which continues to this day.)

Against a background of such expansion, it is easy to see why what might later appear a Papal betrayal caused little real concern in Dublin at the time. Though the *Laudabiliter* of the first-ever English pope, Adrian IV, in 1155 granted 'hereditary possession of Ireland' to England's King Henry II, there could be little real attraction for the Norman king in mounting an attack on a town of scarcely more than 5,000 people, a day's sailing away. Though there was always the possibility that Dublin might again be used as a base for raids on the west coast of England, Henry might well have lived out his days without ever acting on the Pope's 'generosity'. In fact, it took an express invitation from an Irish king finally to make up his mind.

4

ANGLO-NORMAN DUBLIN, 1170–1300

The king of Leinster Diarmuid Mac Murchadha (Dermot MacMurrough) was deposed in 1166 when the king of the neighbouring Breffni managed to persuade Mac Murchadha's subjects to rise up against him. Knowing that he would need allies in his battle for reinstatement, Mac Murchadha decided to approach Henry II with an offer. In return for Henry's assistance in putting him back on his throne, Diarmuid would make the kingdom of Leinster subject to Henry's rule, thereby granting the Norman king a foothold on Irish soil. To cement the bargain, Diarmuid would also grant to the leader of whatever Norman contingent Henry might supply the hand of his eldest daughter, Aoife. The arrangement was not unlike similar ones made by Máel Sechnaill and Máel Mórda with the Ostmen but it was to have much more lasting consequences.

The result of this new arrangement was that Diarmuid returned to Ireland in 1167 and set about gathering support from other disgruntled chieftains for the imminent Norman invasion. The invading armies duly arrived in August 1170. Under the leadership of Richard FitzGilbert de Clare, Lord of Strigoil, better known as Strongbow, they first took the Norse town of Waterford and then proceeded up the coast towards Dublin, at that time under the rule of the Norse King Hasculf. Outside Dublin the Normans were joined by Mac Murchadha's forces and between them, though initially opposed by the king of Connaught Ruaidrí Ua Conchobair (Rory O'Connor), they succeeded in taking Dublin by sneaking a small party inside the walls and butchering everyone they met. Despite the rallying together of many of the Irish kings behind the dispossessed Norse inhabitants, the Anglo-Norman forces under Strongbow and his governor Milo de Cogan managed to hold the town, a prize which English rulers would retain for the next seven and a half centuries.

REMAKING DUBLIN

During the early part of their occupation, the Normans set about fortifying Dublin by rebuilding and extending the older Norse walls, most of which were by now in ruins. With the work well under way, 1172 saw a visit to his new acquisition by Henry II himself. Staying for some three months, the Norman king roomed and entertained Irish kings and chieftains in a wattle and daub palace specially built for the purpose just outside the city walls and close to the site of the Viking *thingmote*. In order to consolidate his grip on the settlement (and to ensure that its future loyalty would be to England and not to descendants of the Norman lords he had helped ensconce), Henry issued the first charter of Dublin in which he famously granted the city to 'my men of Bristol':

... to be inhabited and held by them from him and his heirs, with all liberties and free customs which they have at Bristowa and through his entire land.

Almost as important was Henry's second charter, which exempted Dublin from paying tolls and duties. This magnanimous gesture was designed to guarantee good relationships with the new Bristol settlers, all of them traders and craftsmen, for whom the Dublin exemption was a major attraction. It should be remembered that, at this time, only those belonging to merchant guilds were permitted to practise trades, and membership of merchant guilds was restricted to those who were 'of English name and blood, of honest conversation, and also a free citizen of the city'. Nevertheless, trades flourished and by 1300 there were over forty different professions listed in the register of guilds.

Like other conquerors before him, Henry knew that the key to the success of a city was its trade. But trade, as he would have also known, breeds jealousy and greed. Perhaps fearing the powerful Strongbow or some of the other Anglo-Norman lords, in 1177 he took the added precaution of granting the whole of Ireland to his fourth son John in order that, whatever might happen with his men of Bristol, the new union with England would not be broken.

Whatever about the shift of power to a king outside of the island, the principal result of Henry's two charters was that a mere twenty years after his visit in 1172 Dublin was already growing so fast that a third city charter, granted this time by Prince John, had to be addressed to the citizens 'without the walls and within'. Where Dublin had already begun to spread northwards across the Liffey, now it was also spreading to the west and south, as well as farther eastwards towards the bay. (Those familiar with the south city centre will be interested to note that at this time the bay area reached as far as what is today Merrion Square and, on the north side, as far as the North Strand, hence the name.) Among the signs of the new expansion to the west and south were the beginning of the building, again beyond the walls, of the Collegiate Church of St Patrick, later St Patrick's Cathedral (on an island in the middle of the River Poddle) and the granting by Pope Clement II of the first of Dublin's five 'liberties', or wholly toll-free zones. (In practice, these liberties remained outside of the jurisdiction of the civil authorities until 1860. The area today known as the Coombe was originally the centre of the liberty of the Earl of Meath.)

Though many of these improvements happened under his government, criticism of Prince John was widespread. Still just a teenager when declared Lord of Ireland, Prince John appears to have had the knack of offending people easily. An argument with Pope Clement, for instance, resulted in the excommunication of the whole of Dublin in 1197 (and the whole of England in 1208, by which time John had succeeded his father to the throne). During his period in Dublin, however, he was responsible for a number of improvements. The year 1200, for instance, saw him secure yet a further liberty, that of St Thomas, and in 1204 the construction of the Anglo-Norman Dublin Castle was begun, probably on a site formerly occupied by a *rath*.

However, then as now, not everybody was happy with the rapid expansion of Dublin. Giraldus Cambrensis, or Gerald of Wales, whose famous fact-finding mission to Ireland on behalf of the king in 1183 resulted in the xenophobic *History and Topography of Ireland,* uncharacteristically passes up the opportunity to rubbish it. Gerald of Wales's silence was not, however, the norm. As Dublin continued to make its influence felt ever farther afield, increased hostility from neighbouring Irish clans led to the massacre of five hundred Normans in 1209 in the area around the modern south-side village of Ranelagh, then Cullenswood. The result was an even greater emphasis on patrolling and protecting the boundaries of the city and surrounding territories under Norman rule. In many respects, recurring attacks by the Irish succeeded only in reinforcing the Norman identity of the settlement. Though trade was by now largely confined to one-way traffic from England, their new confidence and relative security encouraged the citizens of Dublin to seek, and gain in 1229, the right to elect their own mayor. Further church institutions followed, the Collegiate Church of St Patrick became St Patrick's Cathedral and the Royal Mint produced the first Dublin coins since Sitric's had appeared back in 997.

If the citizens were in danger of becoming too confident, however, a terrible fire in 1283 which destroyed the vast majority of the wooden buildings, and a famine which followed in 1294, might have warned them that the city was yet a long way from a significant period of peace.

5

LATER MEDIEVAL DUBLIN, 1300–1536

Even before the end of the thirteenth century, the Anglo-Normans (or Old English as they might at this stage be called) were already beginning to feel ill at ease under the eyes of the surrounding native Irish. Though the early years of the century saw the city walls extended to include the increasing number of dwellings on the north side of the Liffey, the citizens, not surprisingly, were disinclined to share their new-found prosperity with their neighbours. Instead they adopted a system of racial segregation, banning Irish dress within the city walls, discouraging the Irish language and generally patrolling their cultural borders.

Or rather, this is what their parliament did. For in fact the greatest threat to the Norman way of life in Dublin came from the Normans themselves, for whom such shibboleths as dress and language were far less important than they were to the crown. While many Norman Dubliners were busy integrating with the locals or were becoming, as the well-known expression has it, 'more Irish than the Irish themselves', the Irish themselves were rapidly getting caught up in the wave of enthusiasm for all things Celtic, a wave figure-headed by the charismatic brother of the King of Scotland.

The arrival of Edward Bruce in 1316 – and his coronation in County Louth as King of Ireland – was important not so much for what, in the end, it failed to achieve against the Normans of Dublin as for how it led to the changing of attitudes within and without the city. Upon his arrival, and following a number of encouragingly successful if minor encounters along the way, Edward made for Dublin. The city's inhabitants, unwilling to take any risk in the face of this seemingly unstoppable Gaelic army, not only destroyed the only bridge over the Liffey, but demolished churches and other buildings for stones with which to strengthen the city walls against him. Learning from history, they also took the precaution of removing potential cover from the advancing armies in the vicinity of Thomas Street – by burning this entire western area to the ground.

Shocked by the citizens' determination, and unable to breach the newly reinforced walls, Edward Bruce retreated. Though his brother Robert came to his assistance in 1317, the necessary surprise and impetus of the assault had been lost. Defeated at the battle of Ratoath that same year, Robert returned to Scotland and the following year Edward was slain at the battle of Faughart in County Louth.

'Apartheid'

Following this display of aggression by its neighbours (the Bruces' armies had numbered as many Irish as Scots in their ranks), the Dublin parliament became even more insistent on its 'apartheid' laws to keep the city free of Gaelic corruption. Nevertheless, the situation was never quite black and white, as it were. While there were laws in place that sought to banish all Irish people who had not been in the city for at least twelve years, strict boundaries between things Norman and Irish were almost impossible to enforce. Many Irish had by now intermarried with the Normans, making it impossible to draw clear lines of division. And the situation was not helped by the general panic which accompanied the arrival of the Black Death in 1347. Wiping out an estimated one third of the port city's population (which had now grown to about 35,000 people), the plague made it virtually impossible to regulate accurately the movements either of long-standing citizens or of newcomers. The 1366 Statute of Kilkenny, prohibiting marriage between Irish and Norman was similarly unable to stem the tide. With wealth and power no longer the province of a select few, the fortunes of the Norman city began seriously to decline. The so-called 'Pale' (that area of effective Anglo-Norman rule some twenty miles wide and thirty miles long, stretching from Dundalk in the north to the Wicklow hills in the south) was rapidly beginning to shrink back to the perimeter of the city itself. Successive raids by Irish chieftains, particularly the O'Byrnes of Wicklow, did little to reassure the crown that even this perimeter would hold.

It was to this dire situation that Richard II of England determined to apply himself. Though king since the age of ten, Richard was never the most commanding of rulers, and some unease must have accompanied him on his visit to Dublin at Christmas 1393. Still, if it was true that the

Irish clans outside the city were now forcing the citizens to hand over protection money, a large army headed by King Richard himself would soon change their tune. But perhaps Richard had never really understood just how intermingled with the Irish his loyal Anglo-Norman or Anglo-Irish subjects had already become, for instead of trying to force an agreement with local chiefs, he opted for the novel but in the end ineffective compromise of the system later called by the Tudors, 'surrender and regrant'.

The idea was that Richard would accept and regrant to the main Irish chieftains their own lands, in this manner gaining their supposed gratitude and unswerving loyalty. Certainly his common sense must be brought into question. That he can really have believed the turbulent O'Neills, O'Connors and O'Briens would so easily be pacified by the return to them of their own lands is difficult to accept, but that he can have believed that other Irish chieftains (many of them Normans) would have approved such bargains, had they been upheld, approaches the incredible. After all, the Normans of Dublin had suffered Irish harassment now for years. Surely they had more right than had their tormentors to expect favours from their king.

In the event it was the citizens of Dublin themselves, led by their mayor John Drake, who finally put paid to the bothersome O'Byrnes. By the beginning of the century, the city was seeing its second major plague in fifty years, its only Liffey-crossing bridge (rebuilt after its destruction in 1316) had collapsed again in 1385 and would not be rebuilt until 1428 (leaving the city effectively cut in half), and back in England, successive kings were more concerned with wars in Scotland and France than they were with the grim reality of life in Dublin. The defeat and wholesale slaughter of troublesome Wicklowmen in 1402, therefore, was intended as a sign to both the neighbouring Irish, and to the king himself, that the days of cowering and protection money were over.

Growing hostility to the crown, and a city in desperate need of repair, then, were what greeted Richard, Duke of York in 1449 on his arrival as the new Lord Lieutenant.

THE WARS OF THE ROSES

The English Wars of the Roses, between the houses of York and Lancaster, affected not only England but Ireland and Dublin. Under the Kildare FitzGeralds, Dublin offered Richard a warm Yorkist welcome, while the Ormonds of Kilkenny, ancient rivals of the FitzGeralds, announced their support for the Lancastrians.

The result of these wars is well known, and the details are outside the scope of this book. Suffice to say that, at the Battle of Bosworth in 1485, Henry Tudor, recently arrived from Brittany, soundly defeated the Yorkists under Richard III, killing the king and becoming in the process Henry VII. Though revolts in England continued until 1497, Henry managed to hold his ramshackle kingdom together.

Not so in Ireland. Having supported the Yorkists under Richard and the Kildares, Dublin was far from content with its new Lancastrian king. Even the appointment as Governor of Ireland of Gearóid Mór FitzGerald, Earl of

Kildare, did little to quell the rising discontent. While Henry might have thought it expedient to appoint as ruler the leader of the strongest clan in the country ('Since all Ireland cannot rule this man, let this man rule all Ireland'), the result was that Dublin became even more of a hot-bed of anti-Englishness and, of course, the ideal base for those who might want to challenge Henry's throne.

THE GREAT PRETENDERS

The first person to challenge Henry VII's claim was Lambert Simnel. The son of a humble Oxford tradesman, Simnel, or so it was claimed, was the rightful heir to the Yorkist crown which Henry had unfairly seized. Despite the fact that Henry was not the only one who suspected Simnel's credentials as Edmund, Earl of Warwick, the citizens of Dublin took him to their hearts and on 24 May 1487 at Christ Church Cathedral, with great ceremony and celebration, Lambert Simnel was crowned King Edward VI of England. He was ten years of age.

The often overlooked Irish invasion of England followed soon afterward. Accompanied by about 4,000 men led by Thomas FitzGerald, Simnel set off across the Irish Sea to take his rightful place on the throne, only to suffer utter defeat at the battle of Stoke. With FitzGerald himself slain on the battlefield, Henry must have looked with pity on the young pretender, for Simnel's life was somehow spared and he found himself working out his days as a kitchen hand in Henry's employ.

If the Lambert Simnel affair was as obviously doomed as it now seems in retrospect, it did not deter, just five years later, the appearance of another young claimant to the throne in the person of the elegantly named Perkin Warbeck. In Warbeck's case, however, the consequence was not unpaid domestic employment but summary execution.

What Henry had learned from these two attempts on his crown was never to take his eyes off Dublin for long. In an attempt to keep himself better informed on activities in the city, he had his new Lord Deputy, Sir Edward Poynings, enact the famous Poynings' Law at a meeting of Parliament, then held in Drogheda, in 1494. The main thrust of the new legislation was that in future all laws passed by the parliament in Ireland had first to gain the approval of the king and his council in England before they might be enforced. In effect this move was designed to reduce the Irish parliament to an antechamber of its English counterpart.

But Henry VII had not yet managed to seize total control. He had yet to find a way to deal decisively with the troublesome, and treacherous, FitzGeralds of Kildare. That would be left to his more famous son.

THE SPLIT WITH ROME

Unable to devote enough time or energy to the problem, because of unrest in England and the fear of further threats to his crown, Henry had no choice but to allow Gearóid Mór FitzGerald and his son Gearóid Óg to remain in effective control as his Irish representatives. However, his son, Henry VIII, eighteen years of age when he succeeded to the throne, would not only break the hold of the

FitzGeralds for ever in 1537, but would introduce another new barrier to good relations between the Irish and the Anglo-Irish of Dublin – that of religion.

With the succession of Henry VIII it must have been clear to the FitzGeralds of Kildare that their time living at once under and outside the rule of the English throne was running out. Having broken with Rome over the Pope's refusal to recognise his marriage to Anne Boleyn (he was already married to Catherine of Aragon, his brother's widow) Henry had by now displayed his independence of spirit on the international stage. His summoning to England of Gearóid Óg, now Earl of Kildare and Lord Deputy of Ireland, in place of his father, must therefore have worried Gearóid and his own son, Thomas. Indeed, when Gearóid Óg FitzGerald travelled to England in 1533 and no word was heard from him for some time, Thomas seems automatically to have assumed foul play. Without stopping to ascertain the facts, Silken Thomas, as he is popularly known, immediately launched himself into a rebellion, storming and taking Dublin, though never managing to take the stoutly defended Dublin Castle. Rejecting everything but unequivocal support for his rebellion, the commander of the rebels had Archbishop John Allen murdered at Artane in north Dublin while he was attempting to escape to England. Such concentration of purpose stood Silken Thomas in good stead for a further sixteen months before crown forces finally managed to capture him. For Henry, Thomas's execution was another unnecessary reminder of the unreliability of the Irish.

The next great change in Dublin life was not, however, to be another revolution or rebellion, or at least not one of an exclusively political nature. Henry VIII's break with the Pope meant that now, more than ever, he had no intention of seeing his power diminished (in either island) through the interference of Rome. If the wealth and power of the church, as evidenced by its monasteries, was not put quickly under control, it might not be possible to predict when or where the next challenge to royal authority would originate.

With religious and political power interwoven to the extent that they amounted almost to the same thing, Henry VIII realised that devoting his energies to religious matters could also yield rich political dividends. As in England, so in Ireland: the solution Henry seized on was the introduction of the Reformation.

6

REFORMATION DUBLIN, 1536–58

Henry VIII's split with the church of Rome might have come about as a direct result of the Pope's refusing him a divorce but, as Henry himself was still a committed Catholic, it represented a schism rather than a heresy. The implications, however, were no less serious.

The appointment in 1535 of George Browne as Archbishop of Dublin was Henry's first emphatic step towards wresting from Rome control of the Irish clergy and its properties. In fact, it was Browne who suggested the Act of Supremacy which the Dublin Parliament of Lord Leonard Grey duly passed in 1536, making Henry head of the Church in Ireland, although Henry was quick to see the worth of such a move. This direct affront to the Pope's authority led, the following year, to the dissolution of the monasteries and the granting of their lands to the various Anglo-Irish earls and lords who were supportive of Henry's new policies. Such a division of monastic lands and wealth was, it must be said, an attractive proposition and made Henry many new friends.

In Dublin, it is interesting to note, Archbishop Browne himself took to acting out Henry's new policies with remarkable vigour, delighting, for instance, in the destruction of the sacred relics of the city's churches in a great public bonfire held in Christ Church Place in 1538.

Religious Upheaval

From having himself proclaimed head of the Church, it was a short step to Henry's being declared 'King of Ireland' by the Dublin parliament in 1541. This in turn led to the Irish earls and lords having to swear an Oath of Allegiance in return for which Henry, as per the old formula, regranted them their own possessions and conferred new titles on them. Unlike similar attempts by Richard II some 150 years earlier, the surrender to and subsequent regranting of lands and titles by Henry proved quite effective, if only in that it succeeded in breaking a tradition of succession to Irish titles that had existed throughout the country for some two thousand years.

Though the Act of Supremacy did much to change political power structures, it was not until 1548, in the reign of Henry's son and successor Edward VI, that Protestantism was proclaimed the official religion of Ireland, with by far the greatest congregation of loyal subjects being in and around the capital city. In the intervening period, Henry had done his best to ensure loyalty among the new Irish clergy, even to the extent of sending over from England his own replacements. This move followed retaliatory action by Pope Paul III as part of Rome's Counter-Reformation. With Europe and England in religious turmoil, the Pope realised that Ireland could yet be his trump card in turning back the tide of religious dissent.

Because Edward was only ten years old when he succeeded to the throne in 1547, government was entrusted to his uncle the Duke of Somerset, who sent Sir Edward Bellingham to Dublin as his Irish representative. Though noted for his hard line with Catholics, Bellingham proved ineffective in curbing the various minor revolts that were plaguing the country, particularly its eastern coast, and he was soon recalled to England. The succession to the throne five years later of Queen Mary, Henry's daughter by Catherine of Aragon, saw the restoration of Roman Catholicism to Ireland and the return of the primacy to Armagh from Dublin, where it had been removed under Edward.

Though a committed Catholic and fervent persecutor of Protestants (a fact which earned her the nickname Bloody Mary), Mary nevertheless viewed the native Irish with great suspicion. In order to prevent further escalation of violence in the country, therefore, it was she who established the first plantations in the midland counties of Laois (Queen's County) and Offaly (King's County). With loyal settlers taking up the offer of free land in the Irish midlands, Mary hoped to extend the reach of the Pale. If such moves did not immediately affect Dublin, they testified to a new royal attitude to Ireland from which Dublin could not hope to be exempt.

7

ELIZABETHAN AND
PRE-CROMWELLIAN DUBLIN, 1558–1649

The succession of Elizabeth to the throne in 1558 saw the prompt re-establishment of the Anglican Church in Ireland, and it eventually led to the establishment of Trinity College in 1592 (for the 'reformation of the barbarism of this rude people'), the first stone being laid on 13 March of that year. Though dogged by the claims of the Catholic Mary Queen of Scots, or Mary Stuart as she was known, Elizabeth managed to resist the numerous attempts to place her rival on the throne and in 1587 had her executed for her part in one such conspiracy.

Despite these troubles in England, and the escalating conflict with the Catholic Spain of Philip II, the reign of Elizabeth saw important developments in the city of Dublin. As well as the building of larger numbers of wooden houses in concentrated areas within the city walls and the erection of the first three public clocks in the country, the first really effective postal system was set up in this period.

While such developments seemed to bode well, the reality was that Elizabeth's appointment of Philip Sydney as Lord Deputy in 1565 and the persecution of Catholics to which he so enthusiastically applied himself meant that there were few real improvements beyond the merely superficial. The Counter-Reformation might have begun with the appearance of David Wolfe SJ, the first-ever Jesuit to set foot in Dublin, but Wolfe's prompt arrest and imprisonment in Dublin Castle did little to convince Catholic inhabitants of the city that any real change was on the way. Even the foundation of Trinity College was more an attempt to curb the practice among Anglo-Irish lords of sending their offspring to be educated in Catholic schools abroad than it was a gesture to the real needs of the population. Indeed, the deaths of 126 people in a freak accident at Winetavern Street in 1597 (the spark from a horseshoe detonated nearby supplies of gunpowder) could serve as a metaphor for the scant regard for human life and living conditions amidst the growing military presence.

THE REBEL EARLS

Perhaps the most important aspect of Elizabeth's reign, however, was the escalation of violent resistance to the Crown. While the period saw the new Lord Deputy George Carew build a hospital on Dame Street and the Jesuits at last gain a foothold in Cook Street (where, surprisingly, they were little interfered with), most of the Crown's energies were directed against the rebel northern lords, O'Neill and O'Donnell.

Having been conferred with the English titles of Earls of Tyrone and Tyrconnell, respectively, Hugh O'Neill and

Red Hugh O'Donnell were, by the time of Elizabeth's succession, the strongest opponents of English power in Ireland. Like the FitzGeralds of Kildare before them, they had shown that the acceptance of English titles was not enough to dampen their drive or independence. Twice captured and imprisoned in Dublin Castle for his activities, O'Donnell had each time made good his escape, and during this period attacks on Dublin from outside the Pale increased in number and strength. The burning by Irish rebels of the Dublin areas of Crumlin and Kilmainham in 1599 led Elizabeth to appoint Robert Devereux, Earl of Essex, as her new Lord Lieutenant. Less than six months later, however, she recalled him on suspicion of collaborating with the dreaded Jesuits. Dublin and Ireland was in a turbulent mood, and it was hard to know exactly who to trust.

Devereux's replacement, Lord Mountjoy, was far more to the Queen's liking. Having executed Devereux for his part in a rebellion in England shortly after his return (suggesting that her earlier suspicions had been well-founded), Elizabeth now needed a representative in Ireland who would quash any subversive energies in Dublin and put an end to the troublesome northern earls. This service Mountjoy performed effectively in 1601 when, with Dublin under close scrutiny, he headed south to Kinsale where the northern earls were awaiting contact with long-promised reinforcements from Catholic Spain.

Though O'Neill would not finally surrender for another two years, the encounter at Kinsale was a decisive one for Mountjoy and the Crown, bringing about an end to large-scale Irish resistance. That O'Neill somehow managed to secure a pardon from Elizabeth's successor, James I (Elizabeth, unbeknown to him, had died three days before his surrender), and that he also managed to retain rights and lands not usually retained by rebels, seems incredible in retrospect. But the death of Mountjoy in 1606 brought to an end the grudging respect afforded O'Neill in England, and must have done much to convince him that his days were numbered.

A BRIEF PERIOD OF GRACE

With the eventual departure from Ireland in 1607 of O'Neill, O'Donnell and ninety-seven others from Lough Swilly in Donegal, effective Gaelic-Irish resistance came to an end. The 'flight of the earls' opened the way for the Plantation of Ulster, designed to prevent the recurrence of Irish rebellions there, and to an escalation in the persecution of Catholics. Under James I, who had seen how those Gaelic lords conferred with English titles and rights could still prove troublesome, even the Catholic Old English were treated in the same fashion as the native Irish, despite their pleas for recognition as a separate category. In fact it wasn't until the succession of James's son as Charles I in 1625 that the Old English were allowed a little more freedom under the so-called 'Graces'.

If anything, Charles and, to an extent, his newly appointed Lord Deputy Sir Thomas Wentworth saw the Catholic Irish as less of a threat to effective government than the new headstrong and non-conformist Scottish Presbyterian planters of Ulster. Though Catholic representation in the Irish Parliament under Wentworth was even further reduced, and the ineffective Parliament certainly posed no threat to the king, Wentworth's championing of it as a model body (one that Westminster might emulate) shows that Irish Catholicism was no longer an automatic reason for suspicion.

A number of improvements to the city of Dublin accompanied the relaxation of the persecution of Catholics. The opening of the first post office at Castle Street, though more likely to profit the administration at Dublin Castle than the illiterate majority of the citizens, was a major step forward, as was the appearance of the first public lighting (by lantern) on the city's streets.

Perhaps most important of all, in terms of the subsequent reputation of Dublin as a home for drama and literature, was the opening in 1637 of the city's first theatre. It was established by John Ogilby in Werburgh Street and was a hugely popular development with everyone but the Puritans who just four years later succeeded in having it shut down. Theatre in Dublin, however, was something that would not be so easily suppressed and, less than twenty years later, in 1661, a second theatre, the Smock Alley Playhouse, opened beside present-day Lower Exchange Street. The Playhouse, or Theatre Royal as it was to become, survived for over a hundred years, and it was here that the first great figures of the Dublin stage, such as Margaret (Peg) Woffington and Thomas Sheridan made their debuts.

The summoning of Wentworth to England and his execution in 1641 (though not, it should be pointed out, for his activities as Lord Deputy) prompted an immediate insurrection in Ireland. The resultant chaos, to some extent aggravated by the English Civil War of the following year, meant that Irish Catholics, joined by the Old English of a number of southern towns, seized the opportunity to form their own effective government, the Confederation of Kilkenny.

DUBLIN AND KILKENNY: A TALE OF TWO CITIES

With the Kilkenny challenge to the Dublin administration, the appointment as Lord Lieutenant in 1643 of James Butler, Earl of Ormond and Ossory, failed to make the much-needed peace between royalist and confederate forces. In fact the one year's truce which Butler managed to establish in September of that year simply afforded the confederate armies of Owen Roe O'Neill more time to prepare themselves for future conflict. This conflict reached a height in 1646 when O'Neill and Thomas Preston laid siege to Dublin, with Ormond only just managing to hold the city.

The arrival in Dublin in June 1647 of 2,000 troops under the command of Colonel Michael Jones signalled direct intervention by parliamentary forces in the chaotic state of affairs in Ireland. Ormond, though left with no choice but to relinquish control of the city to Jones, 'preferred Irish rebels to English ones', as he would put it himself. Accepting his reluctant surrender, Jones determined that there would be no more attempts at bargaining with the Kilkenny confederates. At the same time, however, he did not initiate any direct confrontation. Partly this had to do with the behaviour of his own Roundhead troops who, aggrieved at being removed from relative comfort in Wales, were now generally running amok in Dublin and getting themselves involved in pitched battles in the city streets. Food, too, was scarce in the city and Jones's policy of allowing his men to scavenge and take what they could in the city and surrounding areas led to regular hostilities.

The English parliament's decision the previous January to imprison Charles I and abolish the monarchy had created the chaos in the first instance. Ormond's return from France in 1648 and his efforts to secure the assistance of the Irish confederates for the imprisoned king finally severed the relationship between them and the Papal Nuncio, Giovanni Battista Rinuccini. One of the prime movers in confederate circles, Rinuccini had argued against supporting the Crown at all costs. Now with the confederation falling apart, he left for Rome.

The execution of Charles I followed in January 1649. His son, in exile in France though acting as Charles II, straight away reappointed Ormond as Viceroy, and Ormond, with the support of one-time confederate opponents such as Preston and Castlehaven, almost immediately set out from Kilkenny to Dublin at the head of 1,500 cavalry and 5,000 foot soldiers, picking up a further 4,000 foot soldiers from Drogheda and Dundalk under Inchiquin's command along the way.

Though the army Ormond had gathered was, in theory at least, sufficient to take the ill-defended city he himself had only just managed to defend three years earlier, the new Viceroy was significantly lacking in confidence as he moved first to Finglas on the north side (where he spent a whole month considering his next move), and then to

Ranelagh on the south, the 11,000 soldiers under his command growing ever more restless.

This delaying proved to be Ormond's downfall. A force of some 2,000 foot soldiers arrived from England and strengthened Jones's defensive army, and a clever rumour campaign that additional forces were simultaneously arriving in Munster caused Inchiquin to lead his men south on a false errand, significantly depleting Ormond's troops. Ormond, in turn, made the mistake of sending a hopelessly inadequate number of men to take and try to hold Baggotrath Castle, on present-day Baggot Street, and then beyond the city, hoping gradually to cut off provisions and other links between the city and the sea. He was certainly not expecting Jones and his almost entire company of men to leave the city and storm his position.

Ormond's utter defeat and loss of up to 4,000 men (Jones's figure) at the battle of Rathmines set the stage for the arrival at Ringsend just days later, of one of the most competent – and brutal – military commanders ever to set foot in the country.

8

CROMWELLIAN DUBLIN, 1649–60

The arrival of Oliver Cromwell in Ireland on 15 August 1649 marks a turning point in the country's history. Prior to his arrival, English rule had been largely confined to the Pale, but by Cromwell's time the sense of at least a potential Irish nation had begun to be understood and feared by the Crown. Having repulsed the Scottish invasion of England at Preston in 1648, Cromwell had seen the execution of Charles I and, with the monarchy now disposed of, had set up a republic in its stead. But if the loyalty demanded by him was no longer to the king but to the British Commonwealth, the means of exacting this loyalty were more severe than anything previously experienced in Ireland. Seeing the subjugation of the country as a religious as much as a political crusade, the new Puritan Commander-in-Chief and Lord Lieutenant set about his task of guaranteeing success for the new Protestant land settlements with brutal relish.

At first stabling his horses in St Patrick's Cathedral, within two months of his arrival Cromwell had proceeded in turn northwards to Drogheda, then south to Wexford, massacring the populations of both towns and causing others to surrender immediately before the 12,000 troops at his disposal. While the subjugation of towns and massacre of populations were the most dramatic of his activities, the chasing out of every Catholic landowner in his path 'to Hell or to Connaught' probably had an even greater effect in the long term. In confiscating some fifteen million acres of land from Catholic landowners and redistributing them among his supporters, Cromwell effectively split the country down the middle so guaranteeing that the eastern half would retain for centuries a dependence on and loyalty to England.

Though he stayed in the country a total of only nine months, through the ferocity of his treatment of opponents Oliver Cromwell impressed himself on the Irish psyche as much as on those individuals who had the bad fortune to stand in his way.

Neither would the Cromwell era, if it might be called that, end with Oliver, though it would take an unexpected direction. In 1657, Cromwell himself having refused the title of King to accept the title Lord Protector of the Commonwealth of England, his fourth son, Henry, in Dublin as Commissioner only two years, was made Lord Deputy and expected to enforce the new legislation that required Catholics to deny the primacy of the Pope.

The influence of his father in the previous few years meant that by this time all known priests had been either murdered or deported to the West Indies, but Henry himself lacked the enthusiasm for continuing the persecutions at the level which had made his father's brief visit to the country so memorable. Indeed, though transplantation of Catholics did continue under his government,

Henry was far from supportive of much of the new sectarian legislation (including the controversial Oath of Abjuration) and, where possible, he ignored the rules or bent them to his liking. In fact, with the death of his father in 1658 and the restoration of Charles II two years later, Henry Cromwell would actively petition the new king on the thorny question of the ownership of Irish properties.

9

RESTORATION DUBLIN, 1660–1714

The republican dreams of Oliver Cromwell left the government of Ireland, England and Scotland in disarray. Though the planned invasion of England by Scottish armies loyal to Charles II had failed, Charles escaped to Europe. There, nine years later, and with Cromwell dead, he entered into negotiations with George Monck, the parliamentary general, who helped him word the Declaration of Breda (1660). This proposed a general amnesty and freedom of conscience for those republican members of parliament who had opposed his succession to the throne in place of his executed father. The prompt acceptance by parliament of this declaration led to Charles's return to England in May 1660 as Charles II, King of England, Scotland and Ireland.

With the return of the monarchy, the Church of Ireland was quickly restored and, Ormond being reappointed Lord Lieutenant, serious efforts were made to right the decline of the city of Dublin over the previous decade. The publication of what is arguably the first newspaper in Ireland, *An Account of the Chief Occurrences of Ireland*, in 1660, was an important if short-lived contribution in this context. (Other short-lived contributions would include the *Dublin Newsletter* in 1685 and the *Dublin Intelligence* from Dublin Castle in 1690.) Among the improvements was the laying out by Ormond in 1662 of Phoenix Park. To encourage its use by the city's shooting gentry, Ormond spent a small fortune stocking it with imported deer, partridges and pheasants. The same year saw the first buildings appear on Ormond and Arran Quays, the latter named for Ormond's son. Though it had at first been planned that the buildings should face northwards away from the river, a word from Ormond to Sir Humphrey Jervis led to the buildings being reversed, and eventually to the extensive quayside developments that give Dublin so much of its character. Indeed extensions to the quays proceeded so rapidly that a second bridge (at Watling Street) was added in 1674 and by the time Charles died nine years later the total number of bridges stood at five. Of these, interestingly, Essex Bridge (now generally known as Capel Street Bridge) was often avoided by pedestrians and riders. Not only did it collapse in 1686 after just ten year's service (to be twice rebuilt in the following two centuries) but according to Walter Harris Esq. writing in 1766:

The fate of the undertakers of this bridge was remarkably unlucky; Sir Humphrey Jervis, the first builder, lay in gaol several years, and Mr Robert Mack, a skilful mason, who executed the work to the satisfaction of the public, was a considerable loser, by a mistake in the contract, as well as some untoward accidents.

Whatever 'untoward accidents' might have befallen the builders of bridges, the other major development of this period was the laying out in 1662 of St Stephen's Green, in order that the good citizens of Dublin might be able to 'take the open aire'. Formerly open fields approachable only from Stephen Street or the then 'foule and out of repaire' lane which would eventually become Grafton Street, the Green quickly became the focus of fashionable residential development in the south city, despite the fact that gallows still stood at the Harcourt Street and Merrion Row corners and, according to at least one contemporary report, corpses were often left hanging for days or weeks on end. An anonymous poem from the period paints a very unflattering picture of the city and its inhabitants both:

> Mass-houses, churches, mixt together;
> Streets unpleasant in all weather.
> The church, the four courts, and hell contiguous;
> Castle, College green, and custom-house gibbous . . .

> Women lazy, dirty, drunken, loose;
> Men in labour slow, of wine profuse;
> Many a scheme that the public must rue it:
> This is Dublin, if ye knew it.

Following the surrounding of St Stephen's Green with a wall in 1699 (one of two years for which it is claimed there are records of the burial at St Werburgh's Church of a person named Molly Malone), Francis Aungier, later Lord Longford, was responsible for the development of the lands to the west. Farther west again, other major developments which took place during this period include the building of the Royal Hospital at Kilmainham (today the Irish Museum of Modern Art), modelled on Les Invalides in Paris, and the expansion of the area around the Coombe to accommodate the thousands of Protestant French Huguenots who, fleeing religious persecution in France, had sought a safe haven in Dublin. Their strong presence in the city is attested to by the beautiful Huguenot Cemetery on Merrion Row, off St Stephen's Green, opened in 1693 and the site of an estimated 600 burials. (It is interesting to note that it was these same Huguenot settlers who brought the tradition of weaving and other crafts into Dublin's liberty areas – hence the names Weavers' Square and the Blackpitts, the latter probably referring to large black vats formerly used by tanners. But, then as now, difference was not always something that was embraced in the expanding city, and rivalry between Huguenot weavers and Catholic butchers and meat workers led to regular pitched battles with knives and butchers' hooks. Right into the eighteenth century such battles often completely closed off the quays to public traffic for days on end, and on more than one occasion unlucky victims were found in side streets, hacked to death or hung on railings in a grotesque marking of territories.)

WILLIAM OF ORANGE

The death of Charles II in 1685 and the succession of his Catholic brother James II afforded Catholic Jacobite supporters in Dublin a brief celebration. Though the appointment of the Catholic Richard Talbot as Lord Deputy two years later further raised optimism within the city, opposition to James's rule among Whig and Tory leaders in 1688 led to an invitation being sent to the Dutch Protestant William of Orange to depose James and take the throne for himself. Having completed this mission in England, on 14 June 1690 William, now William III, duly arrived in Ireland and within a month defeated James at the Battle of the Boyne. James having fled to France, once again the position of Catholics worsened and they were subject from 1695 to draconian penal legislation and expulsion from the Irish parliament.

In the twenty-four years which led up to the beginning of the Georgian period, William III and his sister-in-law Queen Anne, who succeeded him in 1702, did little to improve conditions for the once again expanding population of Dublin. (The fifteenth and sixteenth centuries had seen the city's population fall significantly, probably for the first time in its history, due to a combination of famines, fires and diseases. In 1600 the population was somewhere about 10,000 people. One hundred years later, however, it had mushroomed to an estimated 60,000 persons.) Under William, exports of Irish woollen products were banned, causing one of the city's principal industries to fall into sudden decline. And though Anne's father had been the Catholic James II, during her reign increased efforts were made 'to prevent further growth of popery'. Though Jonathan Swift's description of the state of the country at this time seems poetic – 'like the Thorn at Glastonbury, that blossoms in the midst of Winter' – it is well to remember that the decline of Dublin city and the country as a whole was in great part due to a system whereby absentee landlords could remove to England the vast majority of profits from their Irish properties and holdings.

Whatever about Glastonbury, the thorn at Ireland was sharp and potentially dangerous. William III's defeat of James and his harsh treatment of Dublin left him so despised by the capital's citizens that only the establishment of a manned guardhouse right next to his famous equestrian statue in College Green kept it from being torn down. Explosives eventually removed it in 1929.

10

Georgian Dublin, 1714–1830

The city of Dublin was to expand enormously during the 115 years covered by the reigns of the four kings named George, and there is no doubt that many of the city's most notable buildings date from this period, as do the justifiably famous houses with their panelled doors and semi-circular fanlights or transoms to be seen in places like Merrion Square. (Interestingly, the nurseries and children's rooms of large Georgian houses in the vast majority of cases were on the topmost floors, in order to minimise the disruptions caused by young people.) Nevertheless, behind the glamorous façades and apparent prosperity of the Georgian city, a disgruntled citizenry was beginning to emerge and find its voice.

If between 1600 and 1700 the population of Dublin soared from around 10,000 to around 60,000 (a rate of growth never again repeated), by the end of the reign of George IV (1830) it stood at approximately 180,000. The reasons for this phenomenal level of increase are complex but have much to do with the downgrading of agriculture throughout the country and a continued move towards towns and cities in general. Allied to these were what one critic has called 'Dublin's role as national warehouse'. While on its own such a dramatic rise in population seems to suggest a capital city going from strength to strength, the new wealth being created was by no means shared by all of the citizens equally. With the various liberties now greatly run-down and squalid, the gentrification of the city centre, which began with George I, was to a great extent a cosmetic operation, merely masking unpleasant realities with an imported grandeur.

Five years after the succession of the new king to the throne in 1714, the act known as the Sixth of George I declared the right of the English parliament to legislate for Ireland. This, like similar earlier moves, was designed to protect the English system of government against the dissent rapidly growing within the city and the country at large. Just as the early Norman settlers had been quick to intermarry with the Irish, so once again was it impossible to draw a clear line between recent English settlers and their native predecessors. And by the early 1720s Swift had already begun his publishing career, the appearance in 1723 of his caustic *Drapier's Letters* at last giving the city's many and varied dissenters their first really eloquent voice. (The perception that Swift was a champion of the poor and oppressed is, however, fanciful. Despite the generosity of a will which left

> ... *what little wealth he had*
> *To build a house for fools and mad*

in the form of St Patrick's Hospital, the man who considered Dublin beggars to be 'Thieves, Drunkards,

Heathens and Whore-Mongers' was fighting a battle against being consigned to ecclesiastical and political oblivion in Ireland.) His *A Modest Proposal,* which came off the presses in 1729, was an even more shocking indictment of the state of the country, recommending that the food problem could be solved if people would eat children, 'the carcass of a good fat child' being the source of 'four dishes of nutritious meat'. That the first great Irish voice of protest was a Church of Ireland Dean shows that the national debate was already more complicated than the simplistic Catholic versus Protestant argument of popular analysis would allow.

Nevertheless it is true that, from an architectural point of view at least, the Georgian period saw the emergence of Dublin as a city that could stand comparison with its European counterparts. The appearance of the Parliament Buildings at College Green (begun in 1729) was followed by important residential developments on the north side of the Liffey. Under the aegis of Luke Gardiner (d.1755), the banker and property developer, the since neglected area around Henrietta Street rapidly distinguished itself as one of Dublin's more fashionable residential quarters. And while the north side was having a much needed injection (at least as regards aesthetics) the south side too was flourishing. With the establishment in 1731 of the Dublin Society (later the Royal Dublin Society), the city began its relationship with one of its most tireless and productive organisations which, before it moved in the following century to its present address in Ballsbridge, would hold horse shows in the grounds of what is now Leinster House, the seat of the Dáil.

While such advances continued apace over the following decade or so (with the founding of Mercer's Hospital and the building of the Cassels-designed Newbridge and Tyrone Houses) disaffection among Dubliners continued to rise with the increasingly two-tier system in operation in the city. Stately residences within the city confines continued to attract wealthy earls and lords eager to display their privilege, but the common citizens found themselves having to take to the streets to protest against food shortages and intolerable living conditions. One important result of such injustices was that it was no longer only Irish Catholics who were making their grievances known. Apart from Swift, a number of other Church of Ireland clergymen, including the new Bishop of Cloyne, George Berkeley, consecrated at St Paul's in North King Street in 1734, joined in the outcry, demanding equality for Catholics and Protestants, newcomers and native Dubliners alike.

THE 'CLASSICAL' CITY

A growing sense, then, of a Dublin identity was one of the first bequests of the period of Georgian rule in Dublin. The two-tier system was by now undeniable, but so too was the existence of a number of philanthropic organisations that were increasingly active on behalf of the less fortunate. The succession of George II in 1727 promised no great likelihood of a new policy in relation to the city's poor, but events such as the 1742 première of Handel's *Messiah* in Dublin's Musick Hall in Fishamble Street (the fish shambles being the old fish markets) did at least provide some distraction. In fact, so popular was the première that ladies were asked to come without hooped dresses and men without swords in order to conserve space.

While the middle years of George II's rule saw the building of Leinster House for the FitzGeralds, and the founding of St Patrick's Hospital (thanks to Swift's generous bequest), the alarming percentage of stillbirths among the population led to the founding in 1750 by Bartholomew Mosse of the Rotunda Hospital, the first maternity hospital in the world. (The cartographer John Rocque, whose detailed maps of the eighteenth-century city are justifiably famous, estimated the population at this period to be in the vicinity of 96,000 people, though it is likely that it was considerably more.)

Other developments of the time, which included the beginning of the first regular stagecoach service between Belfast and Dublin in 1752, were followed in the succeeding decade by the building of what would become the Viceregal Lodge in the Phoenix Park (nowadays Áras an Uachtaráin, the President's residence), the laying out of Parnell (then Rutland) and Merrion squares and, perhaps most important of all, the establishment of the Wide Streets Commission which undertook the widening of first Parliament Street and then other streets in the city centre, giving Dublin an even more classical aspect.

If the opening at St James's Gate of Guinness's Brewery in 1759 marks the beginning of perhaps the city's most successful industry and most famous product (originally called 'Guinness, black Protestant porter'), this new development also hastened the extension of the Grand Canal to the rear of James's Street and, thirty years later, saw that same waterway connected to the Liffey itself, this new interconnectedness commencing a whole new era of supply and trade links with the country's interior.

POMP AND CIRCUMSTANCE

The next half century or so under George III (the grandson of George II) saw an even greater flowering of development in Dublin, with a particular emphasis on infrastructure. With the laying out of the North and South Circular roads in 1763, the city had for the first time in centuries a sense of geographical definition, increased shortly afterwards by the completion of the South Wall. The sense of a city beginning to enjoy its classical splendour can be seen in a contemporary description of St Stephen's Green and a mayoral assembly therein:

> The inside is a spacious lawn, at the centre of which is a curious equestrian brass statue of his late majesty King George II by Van Nost, around which the several corporations assemble, well accoutred and mounted, to meet the lord major and sheriffs, when they perambulate the city liberties, every third year.

The pomp and circumstance of the occasion is, however, in stark contrast to the fact that in 1764 the same park was used for at least one public burning, that of one Darkey Kelly, a brothel-keeper convicted of murder. The sense of two completely different worlds meeting is also well captured in a short extract from a poem of the time by Thomas Newburgh, entitled 'The Beau Walk, in Stephen's Green'. (The Beau Walk, along the north side of the Green, was a fashionable place for affluent young men to stroll.)

> Mid Trees of stunted Growth, unequal Roes,
> On the coarse Gravel, trip the Belles and Beaus.
> Here, on one Side, extends a length of Street,
> Where Dirt-bespattering Cars and Coaches meet.
> On t'other, in the Ditches lazy Flood,
> Dead Cats and Dogs lie bloated; drench'd in Mud.

Dublin was a city of stark contrasts, and it took a careful and measured step to navigate between them.

The gradual alleviation of the Penal Laws which began in 1778, though it must have helped to increase faith in the city and its institutions, particularly among Catholics, failed to make up for the dwindling fortunes of many local industries now scarcely able to compete with their English counterparts. Though the following years saw the continued widening of streets under the Commission, and the erection of many more fine houses within the city centre (among them Powerscourt and Northland Houses), stiff competition from abroad by the early 1780s saw the area to the west of the city, once home to a thriving community of weavers, become little more than a slum where thousands were unemployed.

Other developments in the city centre at this time also failed to take note of the conditions in which many of the citizens lived. Although the construction of James Gandon's Custom House in 1781 would see the addition of one of the city's most stately buildings, the objections of merchants and dockers (among them the famous Napper Tandy) to its location downriver were simply ignored.

One factor, however, that provided some distraction from the depression of the time was the emergence of the legions of 'bucks' and dandies who ensured that the city had regular punch-ups, wild drinking bouts and duels to gossip about. Sheridan Le Fanu, writing in the middle of the next century, described the Dublin of this general period as follows:

> If London and its environs, with all their protective advantages were, nevertheless, so infested with desperadoes as to render its very streets and most frequented ways perilous to pass through during the hours of night, it is hardly to be wondered at that Dublin, the capital of a rebellious and semi-barbarous country – haunted by hungry adventurers, who had lost everything in the revolutionary wars – with a most notoriously ineffective police and a rash and dissolute aristocracy, with a great deal more money and a great deal less caution than usually fall to the lot of our gentry of the present day – should have been pre-eminently the scene of midnight violence and adventure.

The most famous of these 'hungry adventurers' who used Dublin as a playground was undoubtedly Thomas 'Buck' Whaley, who once walked from Dublin to Jerusalem to win a bet (a purse of the then enormous sum of £20,000), but the activities of his drinking companions were not always quite so innocent, and it was only a blind eye from the law that ignored most of their moral and civil transgressions. (As a short aside, it is interesting to note that another bet around this time was reputedly responsible for the introduction of a word into the English language. A Dublin theatre manager by the name of Daly, the story goes, accepted a wager that he could not introduce a new word into the language. He won the bet by having the letters Q-U-I-Z written on walls throughout the city, thereby guaranteeing that the new word became an instant topic of conversation.)

The rise in this period of Henry Grattan, who entered the Irish parliament in 1775, and his success in 1782 in securing the abolition of the British claim to legislate for Ireland, did much to encourage nationalist sentiment. With its own effective parliament (though one still composed solely of Protestants, few of whom were either interested or active in Irish political circles), Dublin appeared to be on the way to determining its own future. However, Grattan's ultimate failure to prevent the Act of Union of 1800 would see the Irish parliament abolished in that year and the possibility of self-government once again recede.

In the meantime the work of improving the city's infrastructure continued. In a novel set in the period, Sydney Owenson, Lady Morgan, rather dramatically paints the change which occurred during this period:

In the year 1770, when the penal statutes were in all their fearful force, Dublin (some of its aristocratic palaces excepted) was a city full of lanes and alleys, of cribs and dens; whose filthy avenues swarmed with a squalid and mendicant population; and whose trading streets exhibited but a few images to cheer the eye, or to exhilarate the heart. From the year 1782, however, the city rose from its rubbish, and the hovel of mud became a palace of marble.

Nevertheless, the improvements were significant. The widening of Sackville (later O'Connell), D'Olier and Westmoreland streets in 1784, when supplemented by the addition of Carlisle Bridge (later again to be widened and renamed O'Connell Bridge) gave Dublin a new main thoroughfare and one which, for the first time, emphasised the city's north-south rather than east-west axis. (The Liffey now, rather than forming the centre of the city, seemed to traverse it, prompting the central character of John Banim's 1828 novel, *The Anglo-Irish of the Nineteenth Century*, to observe:

Dublin seemed to be equally divided by its quays: a much more interesting as well as convenient arrangement for a city, than that of London, running in parallels, to such a tiring extent . . .

And later in the same book, Banim provides through the eyes of the hero, Gerald Blount, a view of a bayside still alive with trade:

[He] looked over an extensive clustering of the city . . . its spires and domes, its blue roofs and red chimney tops appearing vividly against a background of the sea, of which the sun-tipt waters were alive with vessels, outbound and inbound . . . and he was pleased to reflect how well situated for the purpose of traffic Dublin was; a bay thus running, as it were, almost into her arms.

Until the building of the Carlisle Bridge, of course, the same vessels had been able to sail right up the Liffey as far as Essex Bridge and the Old Custom House on Wellington Quay.

With the building of the Royal Canal in 1789, the city's north side enjoyed much the same infrastructure as the south, the city itself taking on the distinctive eye-shape, familiar from maps and aerial photographs, caused by its curved outer roads, the North and South circulars, and two canals. (Aerial sketches, if not photographs, began to become very popular from shortly after this time, due to the sudden vogue for ballooning, a vogue certainly contributed to by Richard Crosby who, on 19 January 1785, and in front of a crowd of some 20,000 people, became the first person in Ireland to fly in a hot air balloon, though it would not be until 1817 that Crosby's dream of a crossing of the Irish Sea to Holyhead would be realised.)

The Abolition of Parliament, 1800

Over the next few years the laying out of Fitzwilliam Square on the south and Mountjoy on the north side seemed further to suggest an equivalence between the developments on either bank of the Liffey, an equality that was, however, to prove short-lived. While the middle years of George III's reign saw additional developments in the form of Jervis Street Hospital and the Dublin Stock Exchange, as well as the founding of the National Botanic Gardens in the then countryside of Glasnevin in 1795, they also saw the emergence of Theobald Wolfe Tone's revolutionary United Irishmen. Though the United Irishmen's rebellion of 1798 saw no actual fighting on the streets of Dublin, where the authorities' control was complete, the arrest of Tone and others at Lough Swilly where they were attempting to land a French invading party, the appearance in the city of the corpses of hundreds of rebel soldiers, and the news that over 10,000 had died throughout the country as a whole, did much to cement nationalist determination. Because of the magnitude of the horrors, this would be the rebellion future rebels would most often commemorate. (Added to the list of horrors was the death of Tone himself. Having cut his own throat in prison rather than face the firing squad, he took eight days to die of his injuries, joking on his deathbed, 'I find I am but a bad anatomist.')

The period immediately following the rebellion (planned, it is believed, and certainly discussed openly in both Tailors' Hall and the nearby Brazen Head, the latter arguably Dublin's oldest pub) reached its lowest point for nationalists with the execution and deportation of a further 2,000 rebels and with the abolition in 1800 of the Irish Parliament and the passing of the Act of Union.

The importance of the abolition of parliament can hardly be overemphasised, not only for its long-term after-effects (as we shall see) but also for the immediate cloud of depression that descended over the city. The fact that great changes were under way was not lost, for instance, on the many visitors, including the writer Thomas de Quincey, who travelled over from Britain to observe the last historic session of the Irish parliament. But it was what happened after the abolition that had the greatest effect. Though in itself a crushing blow to those who had advocated self-determination, the abolition quickly led to the mass departure of those lords who had over the previous century built up in particular the north side of the city. Certainly there were those, more comfortably off than the average citizen, in whom the changes provoked speculation rather than worry, but these were the exception. Sir James Brooke, one of the major characters of Maria Edgeworth's novel *The Absentee*, written and set in this first decade after the abolition, explains the situation as he sees it to a young acquaintance, recently arrived from London.

'I happened,' continued Sir James, 'to be quartered in Dublin soon after the union took place; and I remember the great but transient change that appeared from the removal of both houses of Parliament: most of the nobility and many of the principal families among the Irish commoners, either hurried in high hopes to London, or retired disgusted and in despair to their houses in the country. Immediately, in Dublin, commerce rose into the vacated seats of rank; wealth rose into the place of birth. New faces and new equipages appeared: people, who had never been heard of before, started into notice, pushed themselves forward, not scrupling to elbow their way even at the Castle . . . So that now,' concluded Sir James, 'you find a society in Dublin composed of a most agreeable and salutary mixture of birth and education, gentility and knowledge, manner and matter . . .'

What some might call the self-made 'new faces' of Dublin wealth, others might have called the *nouveaux riches* or worse. The fact was, of course, that with the lords went the lords' spending power (estimated to have been in excess of the enormous sum of £600,000 per year). With the vast majority of their great estates sold and divided up, and with no one particularly concerned for the living conditions of the new and generally down-at-heel inhabitants who rented those in the worst condition, much of the north side of the city rapidly degenerated into slums.

LIBERTY, EQUALITY, FRATERNITY

With the decline of Dublin now well underway, and the memory of the severe treatment meted out to the 1798 rebels still a cause of great unrest among nationalists, the 1803 rebellion of Robert Emmet can have come as little surprise to the citizens of Dublin. Where Tone had understood that the securing of French assistance was probably the only way a successful rebellion could come about in Ireland, the twenty-five-year-old ex-student of Trinity College was equally aware that lessons had to be learned from the French and their own successful revolution. To this end he travelled to meet with Napoleon and

Talleyrand in order to fine-tune his plans for insurrection.

This insurrection duly took place on 23 July 1803 with the assassination of Lord Chief Justice, Lord Kilwarden in Victor Street, through which Emmet had been on his way to storm Dublin Castle. But whether breakdowns in communication with the French or simply the lack of fire-power was the reason, this second rebellion in only five years saw no further action on the streets. Emmet fled to the Dublin mountains, was arrested, brought back to the city and publicly executed outside St Catherine's Church in Thomas Street on 20 September as a warning to those who might still harbour sympathy for his cause.

Two attempts at rebellion in such a short period left their mark on Dublin nationalists. But they also impressed on the king and the House of Lords at Westminster the vulnerable position of Ireland in the war against France. In order to prevent further French assaults on the country, the year following Emmet's execution saw the beginning of the building of twenty defensive Martello towers along the Dublin coast. The towers were modelled on Corsican fortifications which British forces had great trouble taking during the French Revolutionary Wars, and formed a line which stretched from Balbriggan in the north to Bray in the south. This defensive line included, of course, the tower at Sandycove, for a short time home to James Joyce and eventually to be the setting for the opening scene of his masterpiece, *Ulysses*.

If the next decade saw the development of Dublin continue with the building of the Royal College of Surgeons on St Stephen's Green (on the site of an old Quaker cemetery), the General Post Office in Sackville

Street and the further extension of the Liffey quays, it also saw the construction of the famous Nelson's Pillar in 1808. It is hardly fanciful to suggest that this 134-foot tall construction depicting the 5ft 2in British admiral, was intended not only to celebrate recent English victories in the war against France but, being placed in the middle of the city's main thoroughfare, was to serve as a reminder to French-sympathising Dubliners that they could not hope to escape the scrutiny of the Crown (even if, ironically, that scrutiny came in the form of a one-eyed man).

THE MOVE SOUTH

The physical appearance of Dublin was by now more or less balanced between its north and south sides, whatever about their inequalities in terms of wealth and facilities. The completion in the early years of the nineteenth century of a further three bridges spanning the Liffey (including the pedestrian-only Wellington Bridge, more popularly known as Ha'penny Bridge because of the toll imposed on those wishing to cross it) facilitated the increasing volume of traffic across the city's main river. Wellington Bridge and Quay and the enormous Wellington testimonial obelisk in the Phoenix Park all served to remind Dubliners that it was in their own city that the duke who had finally defeated Napoleon (and so destroyed the hopes of French assistance) had been born.

While the mass withdrawal of lords from Dublin following the Act of Union did much to change the fabric of the north side of the city in particular, the government of Ireland was certainly not ignored at Westminster.

Indeed great efforts were made to ensure no lapse of communication might follow between the two countries, and the building of the new Bull Wall and the new harbour at Kingstown were both intended to facilitate such communication. Though Howth, to the north of the city, had originally been chosen as the site of the mail station, the harbour's rapid deterioration due to accumulation of silt meant that passenger and mail facilities were soon transferred to the south.

CATHOLIC EMANCIPATION

By the end of the reign of George III, the city had undergone enormous changes, though the king's insanity in his last decade or so must have meant that many of the changes had occurred without his knowledge. Among the new buildings that had appeared was St Mary's Pro-Cathedral on Marlborough Street in the north city centre, begun in 1814, it is believed to a design by one John Sweetman that had won a design competition organised by his brother, William. (Given the close relationship between contestant and organiser, the slight doubt probably reflects an intentional blurring of details.) Incidentally, the building was originally intended to stand on the site of the General Post Office (GPO) on O'Connell Street, but in spite of the easing of the Penal Laws it was decided that a less 'provocative' location might be the wiser choice for a Church still regaining its confidence.

The succession to the throne of George III's son in 1820 as George IV might have held out brief hopes for Irish Catholics (George, well known for his independent even occasionally reckless actions, had himself married a Catholic widow in 1785). But if changes were on the way, it would not be the new king but a Kerry-born lawyer who would ring them in.

Called to the Irish Bar in 1798, the year of Wolfe Tone's ill-fated rebellion, Daniel O'Connell had recorded his opposition to the Act of Union in his first public speech in 1800, and his founding of the Catholic Association in 1823 served to clarify his intention of pursuing rights for Catholics. O'Connell's skills as an orator gained him many supporters (despite the fact that he admitted to killing a man, one John d'Esterre, in a duel in Kildare in 1815), and in 1828 as part of his campaign for Catholic emancipation he was elected MP for County Clare. The fact that O'Connell was a Catholic, and a vociferous one at that, led to a great crisis in parliament where Catholics could not take seats. The situation was resolved in 1829 with the passing of the Relief Bill which at last granted Catholic Emancipation and made provision for Catholics to hold civil and military offices.

Though the king's death the following year brought to an end the period of the four Georges, in which Dublin had not only expanded dramatically but had taken on much of its present physical character, it also marked the beginning of a new resolve among the Irish Catholic inhabitants of the city.

11

DUBLIN AND THE GREAT FAMINE, 1840–50

The period prior to Catholic Emancipation had seen administration of the city carried out exclusively by the Protestant minority who made up the ninety-six members of the Common Council, the twenty-five aldermen, two sheriffs and Lord Mayor. However, in the period immediately following the passing of the bill, the Catholic majority moved rapidly into positions of power and influence. Where members of the Common Council had previously been elected from the Protestant-only members of the various trades guilds, the Relief Bill and the Municipal Reform Bill which followed it in 1840 meant that the new city Corporation was elected by all those citizens who paid rates. Considering that an estimated three-quarters of the city's population of 300,000 was Catholic, it is not surprising that the new corporation more truly reflected the actual demographics of the city. With the 1841 election of Daniel O'Connell as Lord Mayor, changes were imminent.

Apart from these sweeping changes in the constitution of Dublin's administration, other changes were also on the way. While 1837 had seen the establishment of the Dublin Metropolitan Police force (drawing on structures put in place by Sir Arthur Wellesley, the Duke of Wellington, some thirty years before), the greatest of the new changes came in the form of the railway system, first introduced to Ireland in 1834 with the laying of a line between Westland Row in Dublin and the mail boat operating out of Kingstown (later to return to its Irish name of Dun Laoghaire). The excitement generated by the appearance of these steam-driven engines is today difficult to imagine but, if the new railways would lead to the building of grand stations at Amiens Street and Kingsbridge, the benefits from rapid and easy trade with the rest of the country did not always fall to the citizens of Dublin. Following the Act of Union and the withdrawal of parliament from the city, trade and manufacture in Dublin had gone into rapid decline, exacerbated by embargoes on exports and by the removal of duties on English-manufactured imports. Despite the fact that they now had the first suburban rail line in the world, the real benefits of greater access to Irish markets fell not to Dublin's manufacturers but to their English competitors.

THE YOUNG IRELANDERS

Against such a background, the 'monster' gatherings organised by Daniel O'Connell in order to bring about the repeal of the Act of Union inevitably led to high spirits and even the possibility of violence among those who doubted the likelihood of constitutional change. The cancellation of a rally at Clontarf in 1843 was the result of such concerns about violence, as was O'Connell's arrest the following year on charges of 'conspiracy' and disturbing the peace. Following a reversal of judgement, O'Connell was released after serving only four months of his twelve-month sentence, but the first appearance of potato blight in September 1845 did little to bridge the ever-widening gap between those who supported his political agitation and those who favoured the increasingly revolutionary Young Irelanders Thomas Davis, William Smith O'Brien and John Mitchel.

Though ten years before O'Brien had himself determined to follow a more moderate path than O'Connell (indeed he had differed greatly with John Mitchel's advocacy of force), by the time of O'Connell's death in 1847, he had come to the conclusion that a rebellion was the only available course of action. With the arrest and deportation to Bermuda of Mitchel earlier that year, following his calls for a 'holy war' on the English in Ireland in the pages of his *United Irishman,* in July 1848 O'Brien was himself arrested and, though sentenced to death, was instead deported to Tasmania. The arrest and imprisonment of other Young Irelanders, among them the Waterford-born lawyer Thomas Francis Meagher, not only led to the necessity of extending Kilmainham jail but, more importantly, led to riots on the streets of Dublin and the subsequent passing of the Crime and Outrage Act.

The efforts of O'Brien and others, not surprisingly, ended in disaster, but they did serve to show the commitment to force still held by Irish nationalists. Nevertheless, if the rebel spirit of the Young Irelanders had been visible to a large extent in the attitudes expressed in Thomas

Davis's *Nation* (a journal to which many of the organisation's most prominent members had contributed since
its appearance in 1842), not all of the Young Irelanders
could be said to have had the same purity of vision as the
paper's founder. While Thomas Francis Meagher ended
up fighting for the Union in the American Civil War and
became Secretary of Montana State in 1865, John
Mitchel's later career as a slave-trader in America must
cast serious doubts on just what kind of emancipation he
had envisioned.

THE BUSINESS OF FAMINE

In the middle years of the nineteenth century, Dublin
was, as all cities are, to a great extent dependent on
foodstuffs supplied by the rest of the country, though it
also had the advantage of proximity to England. The Great
Famine of 1847–9, which resulted from the failure of the
potato crop in 1845 and subsequent years, therefore,
affected the city in very different ways to the rest of the
country. If the dozen or more smaller famines that had
occurred in the forty-five years since the Act of Union
might have shown anything, it was that reliance on a single
crop such as the potato was ill-advised. But though it
should be remembered that the potato was the basic rather
than the sole diet of the majority of people across the
country, its abundance in good years meant that it had
also become the basic ingredient of fodder for pigs, and
so its failure caused a severe break in the food chain.
(Blight, of course, was not the only effect of extreme
weather conditions in the period. Some six years earlier,

on 6 January 1839, hurricanes on the 'Night of the Big Winds' destroyed or significantly damaged more than 5,000 houses in the Dublin region alone.) The importation in 1847 of Indian meal as a substitute for the potato, though more useful than the tardy repeal of the Corn Laws the previous year under Prime Minister Robert Peel, had less and less effect as one moved west from Dublin. What few supplies did make it beyond the east coast and across the Shannon into the hardest-hit areas of Mayo and Galway could do little to appease what historian Roy Foster has called the 'skeletal armies' by then walking the land.

SLUM DWELLINGS AND SOUP KITCHENS

Between 1847, when the Famine began in earnest, and 1851 when the next census was taken, the population of Ireland fell by more than two million due to starvation, disease and emigration. But the period also saw a large-scale migration to the towns, cities and, of course, to the ports. The result of evictions for non-payment of rent, due to the crop failure (the area around Dublin was one of the least affected in the country in this respect) these migrations led to the setting-up of massive soup kitchens for the poor in Merrion Square. Supervised by the French chef Soyer, the kitchens attracted queues of thousands. Claims that the soup contained only vegetables, however, soon led to near riots and Soyer had to flee the country in fear of his life. On a more long-term scale, the massive influx into the city during the Famine years marked the beginning of the great rise in tenement dwellings which was to be such a striking feature of Dublin's inner city over the next 100 years.

The great Georgian buildings which characterise modern Dublin were, as pointed out, the products of an eighteenth- and early nineteenth-century vision. But where the Georgian character of other cities in these islands was added to or considerably altered during the reign of Victoria, which began in 1837, few such changes occurred in Dublin. Primary among the reasons for this was the dire poverty of much of the city in the post-Famine period. The combination of a lack of development since the Act of Union, and the sudden influx of people dispossessed by the effects of the Famine, meant that what buildings there were remained more or less as they stood, the biggest changes coming in the matter of occupancy levels. Though scarcely half a century earlier the houses of the west side of the city and the extended quays had been home to single families, now they were expected to contain the masses of new poor who not only filled them to bursting point, but who also flooded into the Georgian houses on the city's once-fashionable north side. So bad was the situation with overcrowding in 1861 that, according to the census of that year, close to 50 per cent of Dublin families now lived in one-roomed accommodation. In the census of 1798, by comparison, a total of only 100 people inhabited 10 of the largest houses on Mountjoy Square.

Where the first half of the century had seen the appearance of such venerable institutions as the first of Bewley's cafés in Sycamore Alley off Dame Street (1846) and the Royal Irish Academy of Music in Westland Row (1848), the beginning of the second half saw the city facing poverty and squalor of unprecedented levels. In Peter Ackroyd's fictional *The Last Testament of Oscar Wilde*, (1983) set during this time, Oscar looks back on his childhood and decides:

> Dublin was in the fifties and sixties already a decaying city; like an old prostitute, it had long ago lost its virtue and was in danger of losing its income.

Fortunately, the challenge of cleaning itself up was not one which the city would ignore if, too often, it was the citizens themselves and not the civil authorities who rose to the task.

But before the many small charitable organisations then in existence could give birth to the kind of philanthropy which would guarantee Sir Arthur Guinness a place in the heart (as well as the appetite) of the city, yet another new republican organisation had first to emerge from the depression of the post-Famine years to make its bid for change.

12

Fenian Dublin, 1858–67

More or less concurrent with the establishment of a Catholic University at St Stephen's Green in 1854 were the beginnings of a revival of interest in Irish language and culture (particularly literature), carrying and fuelled by the disparate energies which would in 1858 give shape to the Fenian movement. To a great extent the offspring of the failed Young Ireland movement, and containing many of its members, Fenian organisations emerged simultaneously in Dublin and New York, guaranteeing them an international profile. Whereas the Fenian Brotherhood was the name of the organisation founded, for the most part, by those who had fled or been deported after the Young Ireland fiasco, the Irish Republican Brotherhood was essentially the same organisation in Ireland (though, it must be said, of necessity the illegal IRB's activities would remain secret). What united such diverse figures as John O'Mahony, the Kilkenny-born civil engineer James Stephens, Cork grocer Jeremiah O'Donovan Rossa and Tipperary-born medical student John O'Leary (later immortalised by Yeats in his poem 'September 1913') was a commitment to physical force.

In order to bring public opinion to the point where it would support yet another attempt at rebellion, the Fenians (probably for the first time for any Irish republican movement) wholly embraced the media both within the country and abroad. Where the voice of Davis's *Nation* had been confined almost exclusively to Ireland, the journals founded by the Fenians on both sides of the Atlantic now endeavoured to spread the message of Irish republicanism and the inextricably linked cultural revival on as wide a stage as possible. Indeed it could be said that the obviously ill-fated Fenian invasion of Canada in 1866 (the same year as a cholera epidemic devastated Dublin) was in fact the organisation's first major publicity stunt. Certainly Monaghan born John O'Neill can have had few other motives when in June of that year he crossed the Niagara river from America with only 800 men to try to capture a country of over 3,500,000 sq. miles. The statement subsequently issued by the Fenian leaders, 'The Irish Republican Army has been in action for the first time,' seems to bear out this interpretation of events.

While Fenian fervour was still building throughout Ireland and abroad, Dublin itself was experiencing something of a revival, the continued appalling conditions of the tenements temporarily aside. The opening of the new National Gallery on Merrion Square (to which playwright George Bernard Shaw would bequeath one third of his royalties in thanks for his 'education' there), and the appearance of the first issue of *The Irish Times* in 1859 were followed by the laying of the first tram lines in 1861 and the establishment of the Dublin Fire Brigade the following year. The Dublin International Exhibition of 1865 at Earlsfort Terrace, like the Dublin Exhibition of Arts, Industries and Manufacturers which would take place in 1872 on the same site, did much to draw attention to a city rapidly refinding its feet. Though the introduction of gas lighting in the city centre removed some of the gloom that hung over the streets, the new tramways encouraged the better-off to move their places of residence out of the city centre, making fashionable the new suburbs of Rathmines, Donnybrook, Pembroke and Clontarf.

But if recent Irish history was anything to go by, a rebellion by the new generation of republican nationalists could not be far off.

THE FAILURE OF REBELLION

The notion that every successive generation of Irishmen had a duty to rise up against English rule was essentially originated by the Fenians. And if their actions abroad were by times colourful, their determination and resolve at home could not be called into question. So aware, indeed, was James Stephens of the pressures of this duty that, having raised funds in America with the promise of a rising in 1865, and generating support back home through his recently founded newspaper *The Irish People*, he took to a symbolic level the notion of following in the footsteps of rebel predecessors. When it came to setting the date for the latest rising, he chose 20 September, the sixty-fourth anniversary of Robert Emmet's execution. Spurring him on were Emmet's last words in his speech from the dock:

When my country takes her place among the nations of the earth, then, and not till then, let my epitaph be written.

Like the rebellion of Emmet and the rising of the Young Irelanders, however, the Fenian insurrection of 1867 never quite materialised, at least not on the scale foreseen by its organisers. Though boasting a membership in the tens of thousands, the Fenians had suffered a considerable setback in 1865 with the closure of *The Irish People* newspaper and the arrest and imprisonment of many of their leaders. A bungled rescue bid at Clerkenwell jail, and unsuccessful attempts at risings in Munster and at Tallaght in Dublin in February 1867 led to a move within Fenian ranks away from violence and towards separatism.

Although James Stephens in exile in Paris continued to promise and call for a second rising, that rising would not come for another fifty years, being instead preceded by the parliamentary challenges of one of Irish history's most discussed politicians.

13

HOME RULE, 1870–1913

William Butler Yeats was just five years of age when Isaac Butt launched the new Home Rule Movement at Dublin's Rotunda in May 1870. But where the period of Yeats's life would see great changes in his native city, and the poet himself would see the Easter 1916 Rising of Pearse and Connolly as directly linked to the path taken by O'Leary and the Fenians, the path on which Butt now embarked was clouded in difficulty.

A Tory nationalist lawyer who had defended William Smith O'Brien and various other Young Irelanders and Fenians in their trials, Isaac Butt had also opposed Daniel O'Connell's efforts to change the composition of the formerly all-Protestant Dublin Corporation. His call for Home Rule, therefore, is another clear reminder that supporters of constitutional separation were not confined to any one religious or political group. The Home Rule Movement, though it may have taken a few years to make itself felt, was a force behind which a great variety of aspirations were gathered. If by 1873 Catholic suspicion of the movement had abated sufficiently to see its consolidation as a political party (with a sister organisation, the Home Rule Confederation of Great Britain across the sea), not all Catholics or nationalists were yet convinced of its merits. In the background the IRB remained sceptical of constitutional challenges. In 1876 it would eventually withdraw its grudging support altogether.

In the meantime, however, a number of Home Rule candidates had scored decisive points by being elected to parliament. Though Butt himself had been elected in 1871 as MP for Limerick, it was the election of Charles Stewart Parnell in 1875 as MP for Meath that would in the end make all the difference. Wicklow-born and Cambridge-educated, Parnell was a relatively prosperous landowner who had sympathised with the Young Irelanders and who gradually came around to the belief that the time was right for another challenge to Westminster rule. That he so rapidly shot to prominence was as much due to his initial personal strength and charisma as to his later ability to unite factions under a single banner.

Where Butt and the other Irish members at Westminster had been unable to concentrate attentions on the unpopular subject of Ireland, Parnell adopted a simple policy of 'obstruction'. By exercising his right to speak (at very great length) on every single bill that came before it, Parnell intended to obstruct the House so that it was forced to give serious consideration to his Home Rule proposals.

The result of this policy was that by 1877 Parnell had replaced Butt as President of the Home Rule Confederation and two years later became the President of the new Irish National Land League. Realising that Home

Rule needed all the allies it could get, Parnell had seen the importance of building a bridge between the Home Rule movement, the by-now critical and potentially hostile IRB and those who had supported Michael Davitt's Land League of Mayo, an organisation driven by the agrarian discontent in that western county. In accepting the presidency of the Land League, he may have taken a risk in identifying his own parliamentary challenge with more revolutionary methods, but the risk paid off. Only a year later Charles Stewart Parnell became the leader of the Irish Parliamentary Party.

HOME RULE

The fact that Parnell was himself a wealthy landlord, and a Protestant one at that, appealing now to mostly Catholic tenants, was one that further helps to explain his attraction. For middle-of-the-road Catholics, not wishing to draw attention to themselves, he was seen as a respectable option for the airing of grievances. Support for him was also support for peaceful means of resolving problems in some respects exacerbated by the Fenians. Though Parnell was jailed for coercion in 1881, certainly the fact that almost exclusively Catholic tenants raised some £40,000 for him by the time of his release the following year shows that popular opinion was solidly behind him, within and without the walls of Dublin.

In the general election which followed in 1885, Parnell's commitment and tireless agitation was repaid. The Irish Parliamentary Party took 85 seats, forcing a deal with William Gladstone's British Liberals who had fallen precisely 85 seats behind their Conservative rivals. Gladstone, it should be said, was somewhat suspicious of Parnell's links with the IRB (particularly since a splinter group The Invincibles had assassinated the Chief Secretary Lord Frederick Cavendish and the Under-Secretary Thomas H. Burke in the so-called Phoenix Park murders of 1882). However, proof of links between Parnell and the surgical knife-carrying assassins had never been found and Gladstone himself had since come round to favouring the notion of Home Rule.

In the parliamentary vote on the Home Rule Bill which followed in June 1886, however, it was clear that not all the members of the new Parliament shared Gladstone's view. The defeat of the Bill by 342 votes to 313 forced him to turn to the electorate seeking a clear majority. The electorate duly responded to his plight, by voting the Conservatives back into power and effectively burying Home Rule until the following century.

PHILANTHROPY AND DECADENCE

While the drive towards Home Rule had grown in strength, then teetered, then fallen with the scandal of Parnell's adulterous relationship with Kitty O'Shea, the city of Dublin was experiencing perhaps the greatest period of philanthropy in its history. Such philanthropy was not, of course, entirely unconnected to the movement. If Parnell himself couldn't take all the credit for stirring the more privileged into action on behalf of the less fortunate (though his had been, to a great extent, an exemplary role), the decline of Dublin at least generated an awareness among the more wealthy sections of its population that they would have to take a more active role in its running, if it was to survive. Indeed even foreign visitors, like the French writer Pascal Grousset, could see that trouble was brewing on the streets. An extract from his *Ireland's Disease* (published in 1888, the year of the first All-Ireland football final at Clonskeagh, in south Dublin) paints a picture that is alarmingly familiar.

> What gives the principal streets of Dublin their peculiar character is the perpetual presence at every hour of the day of long rows of loiterers . . . As in Naples they stop there by hundreds; some in a sitting position or stretched at full length on the bare stone, others standing with their backs to the wall, all staring vaguely in front of them, doing nothing, hardly saying more . . . absorbed in the dull voluptuousness of inaction.

Though by now in possession of a restored Christ Church Cathedral, a Trinity College which for the first time admitted Roman Catholics to fellowships and offices, and the new Star of Erin Theatre (later the Olympia) which shared prestige with the Gaiety (1871), Dublin still lacked a large public park at its centre. While the Wide Streets Commission had done much to improve the claustrophobic conditions imposed by the earlier narrow, winding streets, the closure in 1814 of St Stephen's Green to all except those who could afford the yearly payment of one guinea provoked Sir Arthur Guinness MP (later Lord Ardilaun) to have the Green returned to the common citizenry through an Act of Parliament in 1877. This visionary move not only gave Dublin one of its finest and most celebrated parks, but ensured that the area would not fall into the hands of developers in our own century.

If his first major bequest was in financing with his own moneys the laying out of the new park, Sir Arthur's philanthropy continued in 1890 with the foundation of the Guinness Trust to provide cheap housing for the city's poorer inhabitants, mostly in the western part of the city. Indeed the philanthropy of the Guinness family continued into the twentieth century with the foundation of the Iveagh Trust, responsible for the building of such amenities as Iveagh House and the public swimming facilities in Bride Street.

Still in the last decade of the nineteenth century, however, the shift of emphasis in the city from the north to the south side continued, leaving behind it only vague memories of the grandeur that had been the areas of Henrietta Street and Mountjoy Square. The removal to and opening of the National Library of Ireland in grand new premises on Kildare Street in 1883, and the found-ation of the National Museum only yards away the following year, made a return of emphasis to the north side increasingly unlikely.

In the years following Parnell's death in 1891 Glad-stone persevered with the Home Rule Bill, having it passed by Commons in September 1893, only to be defeated at the House of Lords seven days later. Back in Dublin tensions ran high, and the build-up to the next attempt at an armed rising was already beginning with the first publication of Arthur Griffith's *United Irishman* in 1899 and the foundation that same year of the Irish Literary Theatre, later to become the Abbey Theatre. Along with the Gaelic League of Douglas Hyde and Eoin MacNeill, founded in 1893, the new Abbey would do much to return the question of Irish language and culture to centre stage in the argument for separation from Westminster.

But as Dublin was entering the twentieth century, with a population now close to half a million, poverty was the norm for at least half of that number, and the appalling living conditions which the north city centre in particular had been suffering for half a century showed no signs of improving. Wide-spread prostitution and gambling, for instance, in the area of Montgomery Street (now Foley Street) then colloquially known as Monto, was ignored by the authorities who must have believed that such avenues of release were necessary in a garrison city. (Tolerance of Monto, whose fame had by now spread throughout Europe, and which was threatening to become something of a tourist attraction in itself, would finally run out in 1923 when the newly formed Legion of Mary, a secular group originally called the Association of Our Lady of Mercy, under the leadership of Dubliner Frank Duff took to the streets and in a matter of weeks effectively closed the area down.)

But back in beginning of the second decade of the century, the heady mix of cultural and social concerns, which for generations had been a backdrop to armed risings and initiatives for political and legal reform, was now being shaped by the emerging force of a new voice for change, the voice of Dublin's workers.

Where the Land League had drawn for the most part on the discontent of the country's tenant farmers, the formation of the Irish Transport and General Workers' Union (ITGWU) in 1909, under the leadership of Jim Larkin, came from a realisation that a similar organisation for the country's workers (most of them now in urban centres) was the next logical step. While rural tenants rejected the inactivity of absentee landlords, the emergence of worker's organisations in Russia and elsewhere showed that cities could do more than just stand by and watch. Spurred on by a desire to improve the deplorable conditions of Dublin tenement life to which most of the city's workers were by now subjected and, of course, to arrest the continual decline in both wages and working conditions, Larkin realised that small-scale strikes achieved only marginal and temporary relief, if indeed they achieved anything at all. The situation called for something on a much greater scale. Larkin's imprisonment in 1910 on a twelve-month sentence only strengthened his resolve to take action.

Provoked by a refusal of the Dublin United Tramways Company (DUTC) to employ ITGWU members, the general strike called by Larkin in 1913 pitted Larkin and his supporters against William Martin Murphy, the most powerful businessman in the city and one who owned not only the DUTC but also the influential *Irish Independent* newspaper. To hold out against the pressures which such a powerful man and his allies could bring to bear on them, the strikers (at first exclusively tram-workers, though these were quickly joined by dockers) had to suffer even more deplorable conditions than previously and, at the same time, see the strike broken again and again by non-union employees with no concept of what was at stake. (Interestingly, one of those same strike-breakers or 'scabs', Matt Talbot, was to become something of a legend. A habitual drunkard when he 'saw the light', he became a famous holy man and ascetic, atoning for his past sins by binding himself in chains and bands of thorns. The city fathers named a new Liffey bridge after him in 1978, the first bridge erected in almost a hundred years.)

Throughout the city, the lockout had tensions running high. The police were called in to smash the strike but, following riots and successive baton charges, the force itself mutinied. The establishment of the Irish Citizen Army by Larkin and James Connolly (the Ulster organiser of the ITGWU), though a tiny force by any standards, further strengthened the workers' hand. Even the re-arrest and imprisonment of Larkin failed to break the deadlock when Connolly stepped in to take his place in what Larkin had called his 'divine mission to create discontent'.

Because the main hold of the ITGWU was Dublin's dockland (though in a short time it provoked strike action among workers in almost all trades across the city), the lockout of 1913 might well have succeeded in cutting the city off from commercial contact with England and forced a capitulation from Murphy. But the failure of the trade union movement in Britain to endorse and support the workers, and the rejection of the strike by dockers in Belfast who saw Connolly's socialism as a stepping stone to Home Rule and thence to separation, meant the lockout was doomed. By the end of the year thousands of

Dubliners were on the brink of starvation. By January of the following year, with no other option open to it, the city was back at work.

Although Asquith's Home Rule legislation in the months just before the lockout failed because of the opposition of the House of Lords, the passing of the bill by the House of Commons in May 1914 (the power of the upper house having been permanently diminished), afforded little time for celebration or consolidation. With the announcement of a state of war between the United Kingdom and Germany looking more and more likely, hopes of further political gain at Westminster went on the back burner. Where Jim Larkin in his dream of workers' solidarity had been let down by his colleagues in the north and in Britain, James Connolly would now watch his beloved proletariat forsake an unprecedented opportunity for rebellion, instead joining with the Crown forces in the coming war in Europe.

14

THE EASTER RISING
AND ITS AFTERMATH, 1916–23

The period between the 1913 lockout and the early months of 1916 was one of considerable activity by members of the National Volunteers. While the Ulster Volunteers in the north were busy importing armaments, in the south too the volunteers were arming themselves. Serious conflict seemed just around the corner. On 26 July 1914 Erskine Childers sailed into Howth harbour on board the *Asgard* with a cargo of rifles and munitions for the National Volunteers. London-born but reared in County Wicklow, Childers, who had not long before aligned himself with the Home Rule movement, was now attempting to bring his considerable military experience in the Boer War to bear on the Irish situation. The resultant riots by sympathisers to the Volunteers, where four civilians were killed and dozens more wounded by the King's Own Scottish Borderers, might have offered little more than a temporary setback to the Volunteers' forward march had it not been for the announcement of war between the United Kingdom and Germany the following month.

With John Redmond, the leader of the Irish Parliamentary Party, calling on the Volunteers to leave their grievance with the Crown aside until the war was over, a split in the ranks quickly followed. The 'pro-war' Volunteers were side-tracked (and ultimately sent to their deaths in the holocaust that was Flanders), but their departure and sacrifice left the way open for their 'anti-war' comrades, now called the 'Irish' Volunteers, and for the closely-linked Irish Republican Brotherhood which boasted a young schoolteacher named Padraic Pearse among its members.

The continuation through 1915 and into 1916 of what many had predicted as a short war in Europe if anything served to strengthen the resolve of the IRB. Growing militancy led to the resignation of Douglas Hyde as president of the Gaelic League in July 1915. His succession by IRB Supreme Council member Tom Clarke, a non-Irish speaker, gave a strong indication of the new change of priorities. By January of the following year the supreme council had decided to opt for as early a date as possible for the planned rising, in order to maximise on the confusion caused by the war in Europe.

In the weeks leading up to the planned rising, however, things began to go wrong. The capture of the *Aud* with a much needed arms shipment from Germany, and the arrest of Roger Casement at Banna Strand in Kerry, did much to undermine confidence among Volunteers around the country. And for those for whom the countermanding order from Eoin MacNeill in mid-April was not a cause of further confusion and frustration, it probably came as something of a relief. With so much going against them, it must have seemed to most Volunteers that the Rising would have to be indefinitely postponed or be a complete disaster. Others, like Terence MacSwiney in Cork, would later regret having followed MacNeill's instructions not to mobilise. On Easter Monday morning the clearly ill-fated Rising went ahead.

As early as August 1915, the lengths to which Padraic Pearse might be prepared to go in his fight for freedom were evident in his graveside oration at the funeral of O'Donovan Rossa at Glasnevin cemetery. 'Life springs from death, and from the graves of patriotic men and women spring living nations,' Pearse said, as if already realising just how much the rising of the following Easter would have to rely on symbolism, and sacrifice, for its effect. For even for the seven signatories to the Proclamation of the Irish Republic (men more carried by enthusiasm for Gaelic League ideology than by belief in the possibility of success) the occupation of the GPO and a handful of other buildings that Easter weekend can have been intended as nothing other than a gesture of defiance, even if in that gesture they would almost certainly lose their lives. The extensive writings of many of the signatories (Pearse, Thomas MacDonagh and Joseph Mary Plunkett were all poets) as well as of Volunteers such as MacSwiney in Cork, had shown that even martyrdom in the insurrection might be an acceptable result. For many, including Pearse and MacSwiney, nationalism and almost fanatical Catholicism would come together in the ultimate sacrifice.

For the few citizens who actually witnessed Pearse's reading of the proclamation outside the General Post Office that quiet Easter Monday morning, the group of men that Connolly, Plunkett and he led up O'Connell Street from Liberty Hall must have must have seemed almost comical. If any of them recognised him, onlookers knew Pearse as an impassioned writer and teacher who, only a few years before, had transferred his highly successful Scoil Éanna in Ranelagh to a larger premises in Rathfarnham in his effort to take on the British education system described by him as 'The Murder Machine'. That he was now standing at the head of a column of armed men seemingly intent on taking over the GPO (as others would take over Boland's Mills in Grand Canal Street, the College of Surgeons on St Stephen's Green and the Four Courts among other major buildings) almost defied belief. Nevertheless, without the 20,000 rifles promised by the Germans with Roger Casement, and with significantly less than 2,000 Volunteers and members of the Citizen Army, the first and last rising of the twentieth century had begun.

It is certain that a large percentage of Dublin public opinion regarded the rebels as traitors who were taking advantage of the war in France (a war to which no small number of fellow Dubliners and Irishmen had committed themselves). Nevertheless, the proceedings at the GPO and other flashpoints attracted small gatherings of the curious: supporters, critics and semi-interested onlookers alike. Also attracted, inevitably, were the gangs of looters who used the occupation of the city centre as a smoke-screen for their own less noble activities. In many ways, it was these same looters who were the only immediate beneficiaries of the rebellion. With freshly arrived troops failing to take from the rebels such positions as the crucial Mount Street Bridge area, by mid-week the decision was taken to shell rebel strongholds from Trinity College and the gunboat *Helga*, rather than risk continuing assaults on the city centre. The result was that by the end of the week the centre of Dublin was in ruins. Little more than a quarter of the buildings the length of O'Connell Street still stood. (Ironically, the winged figure of Victory, which graces the O'Connell monument, to this day has a bullet hole in her right breast.)

EXECUTION

It was not, of course, buildings which were the real casualties of the 1916 Rising. By the time the rebels surrendered, at a council of war in 16 Moore Street, more than 400 were dead and thousands more had been wounded. A significant number of the dead were the victims of a military machine gone mad in streets where excited soldiers, who had expected postings to the European war, fired as indiscriminately as some of the Volunteers themselves had done from their vantage point in the GPO in the first days of its occupation. Indeed, the killing of Francis Sheehy Skeffington, an anti-war campaigner and ex-member of the Irish Citizen Army, following his attempts to prevent looting, did much to bring about a reassessment of the rebels' actions. The imposition of martial law on the city was an additional factor.

The real reassessment, however, came in the first weeks of May. If the British authorities had really understood the meaning of the Rising they should not have proceeded with the execution of fifteen of its leaders, the majority at Kilmainham jail. Though seventy-five others were to have their sentences commuted (among them Éamon de Valera and Michael Collins), the execution of Pearse, Connolly, Clarke and the other twelve was a major factor in the re-emergence of support for the armed cause, support which would fuel the coming War of Independence. (It was not only nationalists, however, who had been impressed by Pearse, as the following post-execution comment from General Blackader, one of his court-martial judges, testifies:

> I have just done one of the hardest tasks I have ever had to do. I have had to condemn to death one of the finest characters I have ever come across. There must be something very wrong in the state of things that makes a man like that a rebel.

(It is interesting also to note that since the rising, the GPO has continued to be the location of the main reviewing stand for national parades and demonstrations, as if successive Irish leaders of all persuasions wished to link themselves symbolically with Pearse's gesture.)

The decision to intern Michael Collins and others towards the end of 1916, was also a bad one, if for different reasons. For it was at the Frognoch detention camp in Wales that Collins began organising his 1,862 companions for the struggle which lay ahead.

The year following the Easter Rising saw renewed attempts to get the movement for Home Rule back on the rails, both in Ireland and in Britain. With the war in France not only continuing but escalating, there was a growing belief at Westminster that the granting of Home Rule might yet provide the carrot necessary to entice Irish Volunteers to enlist. The Irish Convention held in Trinity College that year, called by Lloyd George, was intended to work out such an agreement. But if Lloyd George underestimated the Volunteers, he also significantly underestimated the new Sinn Féin party founded by Arthur Griffith which, under the leadership of Éamon de Valera, was continuing to gain in strength. Following the Prime Minister's threat of a freezing of the Home Rule legislation and, despite the fact that forty-five of its candidates were in prison, Sinn Féin won a landslide victory in the general election of 1918. (An interesting footnote to the rise of Sinn Féin is the fact that the party's name, which means 'we ourselves', was suggested by Máire Butler, cousin of the anti-Home Rule Unionist leader Sir Edward Carson, himself a native of Dublin.)

THE WAR OF INDEPENDENCE

The first meeting of the new Dáil Éireann (Assembly of Ireland) on 1 April 1919 saw Éamon de Valera elected president and within months he was off to canvass support in America. With de Valera taking the political reins, Michael Collins, the Minister for Finance, applied himself to the task of reforming the IRB. In almost all nationalist quarters now, the goal was no longer Home Rule but the establishment of an independent Irish Republic. The belief that half-hearted and badly organised risings and rebellions must be a thing of the past was widespread. Within months the Anglo-Irish war was in full swing, as the burning down of the Custom House in May made clear. Drafted in to oppose the Irish Volunteers, or Old IRA, of whom Collins was now Commander, were the regular British Army, its Auxiliaries and the notorious 'Black and Tans', who got their nickname from their early makeshift khaki and black uniforms.

The most brutal act of the War of Independence in Dublin seems to have been in reprisal for the summary killing earlier that morning of fourteen British secret service agents (known as the Cairo Gang because of their espionage experience in the Middle East), but when armed troops stormed into Croke Park in the middle of a football match between Dublin and Tipperary on the afternoon of Sunday 21 November 1920 and started firing into the panicked crowd, the Auxiliaries entered the demonology of the city. In all, twelve people died (a Tipperary player among them) and dozens more were injured, many of them crushed in the stampede to escape.

The Truce between the British and the IRA on 9 July of the following year brought the Anglo-Irish War (War of Independence) to an end and led to the Anglo-Irish Treaty. But the journey to London by a party led by Michael Collins that October must have been a gloomy one. For already it was clear that the Government of Ireland Act of 1920 (providing, as it did, for separate parliaments for north and south) meant that Collins and the others could not hope for anything other than compromise.

That compromise was duly reached, and on 6 December the Anglo-Irish Treaty was signed, designating twenty-six southern counties as the new Irish Free State and leaving six of the northern counties of Ulster in British hands. The price of this agreement was the retention of three naval bases by Britain and the requirement that members of the Free State parliament take an oath of allegiance to the Crown.

Back in Dublin, however, a motion to accept the terms of the Treaty was passed by a majority of only seven votes (64-57), with de Valera, Cathal Brugha and Austin Stack among its most passionate opponents. Even as the historic handing over of Dublin Castle to the Provisional Government was going on, and the total departure of British troops from the city was commencing, the split in the republican movement widened. Michael Collins may have been Minister for Finance, and Arthur Griffith may have succeeded de Valera as President, but the IRB itself was split, with four of the fifteen members of its Supreme Council declaring themselves to be anti-Treaty. With no one quite sure where others stood, and with half a dozen separate armed groups now in existence, disaster could not be far off.

For Dubliners the War of Independence had given their city the status of capital of the new Irish Free State. For one thing it meant the return of their castle after more than 600 years of occupation. And, most important of all, it meant the departure of British armed troops from the streets. But for many of them, as for de Valera and no small number of others, the concession of the northern counties was too great a price to pay. If the Treaty was not able to deliver, the *post facto* argument went, it should never have been signed. With the War of Independence less than six months over, anti-Treaty feelings were already at boiling point.

THE CIVIL WAR

The first major centre of conflict in Dublin was at the Four Courts which anti-Treaty forces seized in mid-April. Unwilling to risk provoking a British response to the seizure, and no doubt encouraged by the sweeping victory of pro-Treaty Sinn Féin in the recent elections, in late June a counter-attack by the Free State army was launched. Instead of clearing up the situation, however, it heralded the return of warfare to the streets, the civil war which Collins had so much feared. In the shelling which followed, not only were the Four Courts virtually destroyed, so too was the Public Records Office, and with it many of the official records of the country. And with the kind of irony Collins understood, the shelling of his old friends and colleagues had been carried out with artillery he had been forced to borrow from the departing British.

The end of the Civil War came in April 1923 with de Valera's order of a suspension of the Anti-Treatyites' campaign. With hundreds of people dead (including Collins himself, killed in an ambush in west Cork in August 1922), a week after de Valera's arrest by the Free State army, Dubliner William T. Cosgrave, founder of the Cumann na nGaedheal party, formed the new Treaty-supporting government which would remain in office for the next nine years and see something like stability return to the country.

JAMES JOYCE'S ALTERNATIVE HISTORY

If the second and third decades of the twentieth century saw the recurring nationalist dream of independent identity finally realised, in the south at least, another sort of identity was also being forged in Dublin, and one which no history of the city can overlook. Where Yeats was struggling with the identity and place in history of the country as a whole (a struggle recognised by his being awarded the Nobel Prize for Literature in 1923), the identity of the city was being reshaped by a man from Brighton Square, Rathgar, now living in Zürich. Even his beloved Maud Gonne could look at Yeats's terribly serious, even pompous attitude and proclaim, 'Willy was so silly'. But for all the play and experiment in his own work, silly was one adjective that could not be used about Joyce.

Having left what he felt to be the claustrophobia of Dublin in 1904 (on 16 June of which year he had first 'stepped out' with Nora Barnacle, then working in Finn's Hotel, South Leinster Street), James Joyce published his first book *Dubliners* in 1914, the year of the Howth Gun-running and the Bachelor's Walk massacre. His *A Portrait of the Artist as a Young Man* was published in 1916, and his masterpiece, *Ulysses,* coincided with the height of the Civil War. And it is certainly true that much of his writing is concerned with appropriating and remaking the English language so that it might reflect an Irish and particularly a Dublin sensibility, and in this sense the work is that of a revolutionary, albeit a passive one. The irony that the young Joyce had been long unhappy in the Dublin he recorded so intimately and seemed to want to liberate, and that others were glad to see him leave when he did, is evidenced by the fact that in October 1904 a number of acquaintances contributed to paying his one-way fare. 'To free Dublin from his presence,' one recalled, 'seemed very cheap at the price, so most of us heartily subscribed.'

Following that departure, at the age of twenty-four, James Joyce returned to Ireland on only two occasions in thirty-seven years. The second was to follow Nora to Galway where she was visiting, and having failed to write to him back in Trieste. And the first, in 1909, was to Dublin as the manager of the country's first cinema, the Volta in Mary Street, established by a Triestino company. As luck would have it, Joyce's decision to show Italian where the public demand was for American films quickly had the cinema in financial trouble and Joyce went back to Europe. Nevertheless, his brief return to Dublin and attempt to start again there might be seen as an effort towards some kind of healing. His literary recreation of the city from abroad might be seen not just as a declaration of a wounded love but as a pointed criticism of the actions of those who in fighting for Dublin on either side had almost destroyed it. Joyce becomes the memory of the city, even if he cannot bear to live in it. 'He even ran away with himself and became a farsoonerite,' reads one of the more easily approached passages of *Finnegans Wake* (1939), 'saying he would far sooner muddle through the hash of lentils in Europe than meddle with Irrland's split little pea.'

15

DUBLIN AFTER THE CIVIL WAR, 1924–45

The Dublin which emerged from the Civil War was a city of rapid change, and one which drew considerable attention from abroad. With the Royal Dublin Society handing over Leinster House to the Dáil in 1925, the present seat of government was established. The award of the Nobel Prize for Literature to George Bernard Shaw that same year gave Dublin its second laureate in only two years. (Incidentally, Shaw's good fortune attracted, as presumably did the good fortune of the others, the inevitable begging letters, in his case including one from a bank-manager cousin in Ranelagh seeking contributions towards the building of an orphanage, to which Shaw replied: 'Dear Sir, When I was young and poor I appeared to have no relations. I did very well without them.')

Despite a repeat of 1907's notorious Abbey riots (caused, it was claimed, by the mention of an item of women's underwear on stage) in February 1926, perhaps because in *The Plough and the Stars* the playwright Sean O'Casey had depicted a prostitute on stage, the often controversial reputation of literary Dublin was established. Small consolation to O'Casey, who was so distressed by the treatment he later received that he left Ireland, forbidding even his remains to be returned after his death.

Within five years Dublin had the new Gate Theatre, founded by Hilton Edwards and Micheál Mac Liammóir, a new Peacock Theatre for experimental work, and was the home of 2RN, the country's first radio station, operating from beside the GPO and officially opened by President Douglas Hyde in January 1926. (The station's call sign came from the last words of a popular song of the time, 'Come Back to Erin'.) On the social scene, the opening of Bewley's famous coffee house on Grafton Street granted the city what might be called its unofficial academy of letters. It should be remembered, of course, that the real Irish Academy of Letters, founded by Yeats and Shaw in 1931, had at least two abstainers in the persons of O'Casey and Joyce. Where Yeats seems to have forgiven the city in which he had no more than a plate of sausages to celebrate his Nobel award, neither Joyce nor O'Casey were to be so forgiving or forgetting (and Joyce, of course, had publicly attacked Yeats and the Abbey Theatre for what he called their 'surrender to the popular will').

On a very different plane but also arising out of this struggle to forge identity in a new world, forgiving and forgetting were also markedly lacking in Booterstown, County Dublin on 10 July 1927 when the Vice-President of the Executive Council and Minister for Justice Kevin O'Higgins was set upon and gunned down by three assailants. Though mortally wounded, O'Higgins had time to recognise the reason for his assassination (his part in the execution of seventy-seven Republican prisoners between 1922 and 1923) and, according to at least one of the three questioned, told his killers: 'There's been too much killing in our country. The killing has got to stop. You're wrong but I forgive you.' Although the Civil War was already four years over, this was surely its last atrocity.

CATHOLIC NATIONALISM OF THE 1930S

At the time of the thirty-first Eucharistic Congress which was held in Dublin in 1932, a new type of fervour emerged. With some of the largest crowds ever to gather in the city (close to one million for the Phoenix Park Mass of the Papal Legate, Cardinal Lauri), the association between Roman Catholicism and the republicanism of Éamon de Valera was widely perceived and led to his Fianna Fáil (Soldiers of Destiny) party being elected to government and to de Valera himself becoming Taoiseach, a position he would retain for the next sixteen years. (Symbolically, one of his first acts was the abolition of the controversial oath of allegiance to the British sovereign.)

Those sixteen years, however, were not without their troubles, or without the threat of violence returning to Dublin streets. The demonstrations of General Eoin O'Duffy's Blueshirts at the Mansion House in 1933 considerably angered those citizens who sensed that his Army Comrades Association was heading towards fascism. (In the event the 150 republicans who went with Frank Ryan to join the anti-Franco International Brigade in 1936 stayed in Spain until the end of 1938, with the loss of almost fifty of their number, while O'Duffy's Irish Brigade of some 700 were back after only six months.) Against a background of such tensions, an IRA raid on the Magazine Fort in the Phoenix Park at Christmas 1939 brought back the risk of renewed violence on the streets.

THE 'EMERGENCY' IN DUBLIN

In other ways Dublin was not only relatively stable during the late 1930s and early 1940s but was enjoying an increase in communication with the rest of the world. The return of the ports to Irish control came in 1938 and the opening of Dublin Airport followed two years later. With the start of World War II in 1939 – in neutral Ireland referred to as the 'Emergency' – the British Government had feared the possibility of de Valera's neutral Ireland taking the German side, but must have been somewhat reassured by the response of units of the Dublin Fire Brigade to the German bombing of Belfast in 1941. Though the Emergency itself occasioned much plotting on the part of the IRA to secure German weapons and armed assistance, the real consequences of the war were felt by those Dubliners who had enlisted in the British Army and, of course, by the thirty-seven people killed and the 500 left homeless when German bombs were accidentally dropped on the North Strand in May 1941. (For this disaster the German government paid compensation of £327,000 in 1958.)

By the end of the war in 1945, Churchill's suspicions as to the motives of the government of Éire appeared to have been borne out by de Valera's visit to the German Embassy to express formal condolences on Hitler's death and by the Taoiseach's response to Churchill's criticism:

Mr Churchill is proud of Britain's stand alone after France had fallen and before America entered the war. Could he not find in his heart the generosity to acknowledge that there is a small nation that stood alone, not for one year or two, but for several hundred years against aggression . . . ?

If, however, suspicions would remain for some time to come (and if some offence was sure to be taken as a result of symbolic gestures such as the removal in 1948 of a famous statue of Queen Victoria from the centre of the old second city of the Empire), the passing of the Ireland Act at Westminster the following year marked the beginning of a 'special relationship' between the UK and the new Republic of Ireland, the new leader of which, John A Costello, now publicly vowed to 'take the gun out of Irish politics'.

16

DESTRUCTION AND REDEVELOPMENT: DUBLIN FROM THE 1950S TO THE 1970S

Though not directly involved in the World War II, Ireland as a whole suffered through the 1940s and post-war 1950s. While the war itself had occasioned bread-, tea- and petrol-rationing (with the result that bicycles had become highly prized possessions and were increasingly among those items reported stolen), the decade following it was one of doubt and depression from which Dublin, the once second city of the British Empire, could not hope to be immune.

As if struggling to contain the winds of change that would inevitably blow through Irish society after such enormous international upheavals, the Irish government's strict censorship policy meant that many of the authors whose images are now synonymous with the city and country actually had their work banned in this period. Of those included in one modern poster depicting Dublin writers, all but two were banned, including George Bernard Shaw, Brendan Behan (a self-confessed 'drinker with a writing problem'), Sean O'Casey and Samuel Beckett. Prose writers Frank O'Connor, Sean O'Faolain and Edna O'Brien were also among the banned, as famously was American-born J. P. Donleavy whose bawdy novel *The Ginger Man* has the dubious distinction of having been banned, not just once but twice, first in 1956 and then again in 1969. (James Joyce, interestingly, was never officially banned, partly because his books were neither published nor easily available here.)

As the country seemed to be resisting change from within, it was certainly at the same time suspicious of outside influence, as is clear from the banning of many of the greatest international writers in history including Voltaire, Balzac, Proust and Flaubert, calling to mind the words of Oscar Wilde: 'The books that the world calls immoral are the books that show the world its own shame.'

The attempt to freeze the country's intellectual expansion to what it might have been in some mythical past of saints and scholars was in direct contrast to the rapid geographical expansion of Dublin city, the post-war period seeing the beginning of migrations on a massive scale away from the decaying city centre and into new suburbs. Estates like Crumlin on the south side, already begun in the 1920s and further expanded in 1935 (the centre of the development taking the shape of a cross in honour of the Eucharistic Congress of 1932) would soon find themselves part of the city as the green fields all around them, right back up to the foothills of the Dublin mountains, were developed at a rate that alarmed many social planners.

Meanwhile the centre deteriorated. The description in The *Red and the Green* by Dublin-born novelist Iris Murdoch of 'Those squared, cliff-like, blackened Dublin streets' may not have been written about this period but is certainly a fitting description. Development would come, and come apace, but in the meantime decay ruled. (One of the disadvantages of Dublin's not being bombed during the war, according to some commentators, is that the old water pipes under the streets were not destroyed, as they were in many British cities, with the result that they were never replaced or upgraded from their original condition. Some estimates suggest that loss due to leakages now accounts for approximately one third of the entire volume of water passing through the city's system.)

The failure of a much promised bright new era (the notional 'sunny day' popularised by Vera Lynn) to follow the war resulted in a combination of anger and depression throughout western Europe. In Dublin, as elsewhere, badly paid workers took to the streets, and successive strikes played havoc with a number of industries, including newspapers and public transport. Unrest was in the air. The exploding of the Gough Monument in the Phoenix Park in 1957, like the exploding of Nelson's Pillar in O'Connell Street a decade later (during the fiftieth anniversary of the 1916 Rising), was a reminder that the days of settling grievances by force were not yet in the past. (The destruction of the Gough statue, incidentally, has left Dublin as the only European capital without a single surviving equestrian statue on public view.) But by the time of the O'Connell Street bomb in 1966, which did more damage to the surrounding streets than to the pillar itself, Dublin was already on the way to becoming an almost unrecognisable place.

The advent of Irish television in 1961 held up a new kind of mirror to the country and to the city of Dublin in particular. (It is difficult now to believe that as late as 1954 judicial executions could still be carried out in this country, Michael Manning being the last person to be hanged in Mountjoy jail on the 20 April of that year.) The arrival of the most popular form of mass media in the twentieth century brought enormous changes. Formed in 1952, Bord Fáilte, the Dublin-based Irish Tourist Board, could now attempt to capitalise on the new-found international interest in Ireland following its entry into the United Nations in 1955, its joining of UNESCO in 1961 and, in 1963, the visit of US President John F. Kennedy in what would prove to be the year of his assassination. In the late 1950s and early 1960s it would still have been unremarkable to see cattle driven in a leisurely fashion through the centre of Donnybrook, nowadays one of the city's busiest village centres. But Dublin was already entering a period of growth that would be without parallel in its history.

The remark that 'There was no sex in Ireland before television' has been attributed to the late Oliver J Flanagan, the long-serving TD for Laois-Offaly, who after nine years as an independent joined Fine Gael in 1952, and it is true that the new medium did much to alter the country's perception of the world and of itself. For one thing it brought the graphic horrors of violence and destruction into the home, which was one of the reasons why the UVF chose to detonate a bomb in the headquarters of RTÉ in Donnybrook in August 1969, an act of terrorism which previously would have been directed at a newspaper office or public building. A return of violence to the streets of Dublin resulted in the burning down of the British Embassy in February 1972, and the city was to see other car bombs with attendant fatalities over the next few years.

But if the dominant images of this period are of destruction and chaos, the popular and wholesome images conveyed by the new national media and tourist organisations seem today alarmingly close to the 'comely maidens' of de Valera's visions. While the 1950s may have had about them a (greatly exaggerated) sense of innocence and promise, in tandem with the rise of showbands and the boom in popularity of non-alcoholic dance halls and ballrooms (in Dublin as well as across the country), the 1960s and early 1970s also saw the emergence of the new 'gombeen' magnates, men whose inherited anger was increasingly turned on the fabric of the city itself. Though by now many of the policies of organisations such as Douglas Hyde's Gaelic League had been put into effect (including the erection of bilingual street signs in most areas and the introduction of compulsory Irish in schools), the 'customising' of the city was not sufficient to protect its Georgian grandeur from the new developers. With no one to stop them, the bulldozers moved in.

One aspect of the post-colonial experience, reflected elsewhere, is the desire to erase reminders of the colonial power. In Dublin, along with the removal and destruction of statues, this led to the destruction of some of the finest buildings in the city, despite the fact that many of these had actually been the work of Irish people and, of course, had played important parts in the complex story of Dublin. Arguments on historical or aesthetic grounds were simply ignored. In 1965, for instance, almost one whole side of Lower Fitzwilliam Street (sixteen houses) was levelled for the building of a new headquarters for the ESB, destroying one of the finest and longest continuous Georgian street-scapes in these islands. And where the bulldozers failed to penetrate, dereliction completed the work in only a slightly longer period.

The undisguised attempt to erase Dublin's colonial past resulted in the erasure of much of the history of the city's working class, as well as of its professional class and gentry. The loss of this heritage might be understood as an unfortunate side-effect of a desire to make 'something of ourselves' – understood though hardly condoned – were it not for the fact that a similar but even more wanton destruction would continue into and right through the 1970s and early 1980s.

WOOD QUAY

As the name implies, originally a fifteenth-century wooden quay, though totally rebuilt in stone in the late seventeenth century, Wood Quay on the south banks of the Liffey is long believed to be one of the oldest settled areas in the city. In November 1969 that view was borne out when an archaeological dig, conducted by the National Museum of Ireland, unearthed over 3,000 artefacts believed to be of Viking origin. Among these were the almost complete hulls of a number of boats, a wide range of cooking utensils and building tools, and a variety of skeletal remains including those of a young man. Inspections by national and international teams of archaeologists and other interested groups, including city councillors from a number of other European countries, declared the site of the excavations to be of immense international significance, and efforts to have the entire area immediately designated a national monument began in earnest. (Worries occasioned by the fact that Dublin City Council had, for more than twenty years, plans to develop the area for new civic offices, created the understandable sense of urgency.)

However, despite pledges from the government in November 1973 that all development in the area should cease 'pending consultation and further investigation', against popular opinion this decision was reversed the following year. Promises made by the Dublin City authorities that the area would be fully excavated before any building might take place there seemed less and less likely to be honoured, so, under the leadership of F. X. Martin, Augustinian friar and Professor of Medieval History at UCD, a group calling itself The Friends of Medieval Dublin was formed in 1976 to attempt to do what national and local politicians would not or could not. A successful bid in the High Court in 1978 led to some of the area being declared a national monument but did not, however, hold back the diggers, nor did the public demonstrations of that same year which saw up to 20,000 people take to the streets to oppose the development.

The failure of the protests of so many citizens beggars belief. If factors such as rising unemployment, bombs in the streets, and the frequent strikes of this period had not broken the morale of the city, that job was almost achieved by its own developers in the name of progress as they ploughed through the site which had come to symbolise the struggle between wilful ignorance and imagination. (That lessons were not completely learned then is clear from the fact that, even as late as 1997, some of the oldest and listed buildings in the nearby Essex Street area were allowed to disappear, almost literally, overnight.)

While one city was being demolished, or simply left to crumble, however, another was being built. The appearance in 1964 of the city's only 'skyscraper' (so far), the seventeen-storey Liberty Hall on the north quays, shocked many who felt its stark profile had no place in the vicinity of James Gandon's elegant Custom House. Whether for aesthetic or security reasons, however (the building was bombed in 1972, hence its present mirrored appearance) to date there has not been a single serious challenger on the skyline.

In early 1999 plans to revitalise the general docklands area, and in particular to build an enormous new business and conference complex on the north quays drew complaints from locals opposed to any further high rise developments in the area. Whether Liberty Hall will remain alone on the skyline for long remains to be seen.

THE LITERARY CITY

Still in the late 1960s, the city's north side received two further injections of life, even rebirth, in the forms of the Garden of Remembrance on Parnell Square in 1966 and the rebuilding of the Abbey Theatre that same year, to a design by architect Michael Scott (also responsible for the city's first modern purpose-built office block and bus station, Busáras in 1953). Phoenix-like though the re-emergence of the Abbey was, after the burning down of the original building fifteen years earlier, it did not herald a literary revival, at least not for the generation of writers most closely associated with Irish writing in this century. In the very year of the Abbey's reopening, in fact, the country's premier humorist Brian O'Nolan (aka Flann O'Brien, aka Myles na gCopaleen) died. The following year perhaps the city's most celebrated (non-local) poet, Patrick Kavanagh, also passed away. In a period when the city was making some of its strongest and most positive architectural statements since independence, another era was coming to an end, and a difficult one it had been for writers and artists.

The opening of the new library at Trinity College in July 1967, performed by President Éamon de Valera, might have been seen as a symbol of better relations to come between the Protestant university and its largely Catholic hinterland but it would be another three years before the Catholic Church dropped its proviso which required Catholics intending to study at the university to first receive permission from their bishop. The then Catholic Bishop of Dublin and Primate of Ireland, Dr John Charles McQuaid, was certainly clear about where he stood on the issue, having declared attendance without sanction at the university a 'mortal sin'. Ironically, a growing tendency to believe that repressive laws and rules were finally being relaxed in Irish society was that same week dealt a significant blow when an amendment to the Censorship of Publications Act removed the ban only on those books which had been proscribed for more than twelve years.

Though no book was banned for criticising Dublin, many of the literary works of this period, as of earlier periods, cast a cold eye on the city. For whatever reason, the truth is that, despite being the home to so many writers, and more Nobel prize winners than any city of comparable size in the world, the city of Dublin seems to attract more criticism than praise. The Belfast-born poet Louis MacNeice, for instance, opens his long poem 'Dublin' with the not terribly appealing:

> *Grey brick upon brick,*
> *Declamatory bronze*
> *On sombre pedestals...*

although this and other grim portraits are as nothing compared to James Plunkett's novel *Strumpet City* (1969), set around the time of the 1913 lockout, in which we are reminded that not all of those raised on plinths above the level of the ordinary citizens lead perfect lives. In O'Connell Street, for example, as one of Plunkett's characters informs us, we find: 'Parnell at the top – an adulterer . . . Nelson in the middle – another adulterer. And at the end O'Connell – a notorious wencher.' (W. B. Yeats, too, had a similar opinion, at least of O'Connell. In a Seanad debate on divorce in 1925 he reminded his listeners: 'It was said about O'Connell in his own day, that you could not throw a stick over a workhouse wall without hitting one of his children.') Rashers Tierney, a talkative tramp and one of the most sympathetically drawn characters of Plunkett's novel, perhaps puts it best and most succinctly, calling the city a 'glorified kip', thereby expressing the quintessential love/hate relationship which so many Dubliners have with their native place.

Not, of course, that all of Dublin's critics have been Dublin-born. The poet Kavanagh is a famous example of a blow-in, and the novelist George Moore, who in his own words 'came to give Ireland back her language', settled in the city only when he was almost fifty. Half a century of living elsewhere in Ireland and abroad had not made Moore enamoured of Dublin, however, where in 1882 he found 'broken pavements, unpainted hall-doors, rusty area railings' and all manner of other decay, even on fashionable Merrion Square and, up near Dublin Castle,

> . . . shops where old clothes rot in fetid confusion, shops exhaling the rancid odours of decaying vegetables, shops dingy with rusting iron and cracked china . . .

Novelists Somerville and Ross echoed Moore's sentiments, though by 1894 the striking mess which had shocked him appears to them merely monotonous: 'Few towns are duller out of season than Dublin,' reads a passage in their *The Real Charlotte* (1894), 'but the dullness of its north side neither waxes nor wanes; it is immutable, unchangeable, fixed as the stars.'

The stars of the 1950s' and 1960s' literary firmament were at least as critical of the city as their predecessors, possibly because they had been hurt by it and by the atmosphere of censorship and begrudgery which prevailed in their time. Even the gradual recognition of genius which had been afforded to James Joyce tended to leave other writers unhappy. Brian O'Nolan, one of the country's most profoundly original and inventive writers, whose achievements have been eclipsed by those of Joyce, exacted his subtle and playful revenge by creating in his novel (written as by Flann O'Brien) *The Dalkey Archive* (1964) a minor character named James Joyce. (Joyce, an ignorant barman, knows nothing about *Ulysses* and dreams only of some day joining the Jesuits.) Kavanagh, the third member of the major 1960s triumvirate that included the IRA bomber turned playwright Brendan Behan, though capable of great spiritual insight was for the most part so lost in Dublin he never really forgave it for not being his native Inniskeen. (Drinkers in one city centre literary pub like to recall the day the drunken Kavanagh tried to get the attention of ex-GI and wit Kevin Monahan by shouting at him the length of the bar, 'Monahan! Monahan!' to which the dapper American replied, 'Are you talking to me, Paddy, or are you just homesick?') Only Samuel Beckett, in 1969 the city's third Nobel Prize for Literature laureate (Seamus Heaney would be the fourth Irish laureate in 1995) like Joyce seemed to see the benefit of exile, and even he still showed the signs of hurt on occasion. Murphy, the central character of his novel of the same name, hints at what the great novelist and playwright thought of much of the Dublin literary scene when he requests in his will that his ashes be returned to Dublin – to be flushed down the toilet of the Abbey Theatre!

Throughout this period the ballroom craze continued, offering the huge numbers of country people (jokingly known as 'culchies') some flavour of what they had left behind on moving to Dublin. The reluctance or inability of many of them to integrate into city life could still be seen, however, twenty years later as popular novelist Maeve Binchy would observe in her novel *The Lilac Bus* (1984):

> All over Dublin people got on buses on Friday night to go home to great dances in the country. It had been a revolution, they said – culchies choosing to go home because the crack was better there than in Dublin.

Nevertheless, in the world of music and the arts in general, Dublin was improving, and beginning to be conscious of the international role it would eventually assume. Towards the end of 1967, the international art exhibition, ROSC, opened for the first time at the RDS and would do so again approximately every five years up to 1980. Only a couple of days before the opening the unveiling of the remarkably stark statue of Theobald Wolfe Tone had taken place on the Merrion Row corner of St Stephen's Green. (This statue was blown in half in 1971, to be repaired and re-erected some days later.) Kavanagh, whose death occurred not long afterwards, left a few words immortalising an area not far away, words which now took on an extra poignancy:

> *If ever you go to Dublin town*
> *In a hundred years or so*
> *Inquire for me in Baggot Street*
> *And what I was like to know.*

17

'One Advantage':
Dublin in the 1970s

Even a single year of the early 1970s would make a great difference to the appearance of Kavanagh's 'Dublin town'. Back in April 1968, when a huge throng attended a public meeting at the Mansion House to try to halt the intended closure of the Grand Canal ('so stilly,/Greeny at the heart of summer', as Kavanagh had it), it was clear that calm reflection was unlikely to be the prevailing mood of the coming decade.

Strikes and public demonstrations of all kinds took place throughout the 1970s and thereby shaped the decade, as if a frustration with the status quo, along with the influence of people power and the student riots of the 1960s elsewhere, was making itself felt. Within a couple of months of the first civil rights marches in Derry in 1968, thousands of students took to the streets of Dublin to protest the lack of sufficient grant aid; then within months successive strikes by Corporation workers, firemen, maintenance workers, secondary and primary teachers, and a whole host of others, followed. In February 1974 the first-ever strike in its 215-year history brought fitters at the Guinness Brewery to the gates.

The last CIE dray horse was retired in 1968, and the city's first parking metres were introduced in early 1970, an indication that the era of transport and traffic problems had begun in earnest. The increase in traffic, although obvious even then, was not given sufficient attention, leaving today's Dubliners and visitors with a suspicion that the inconveniences of the old system (dirt, smells and lack of speed) differed only in kind from those of the new.

Indeed, traffic has been the other half of the planning nightmare of Dublin which, if it did not actually begin in the 1970s, certainly took on new meaning from that time. So much so that the words of Dublin surgeon and writer Oliver St John Gogarty (the model for Joyce's Buck Mulligan in *Ulysses*) seem now doubly ironic. 'Dublin has one advantage,' he wrote in his memoir *As I Was Going Down Sackville Street*, in 1937, 'it is easy to get out of it.'

Plans ranging from passenger barges on the Liffey (abandoned because of low bridges and high tides) to the reintroduction of trams jostled for headlines in the city's three daily and two evening newspapers throughout the 1970s and into the 1980s but traffic solutions were as far away as solutions to the problem of development. As at Wood Quay, people's aspirations did not necessarily add up to people power.

Four Georgian houses on the corner of Hume Street and St Stephen's Green, for instance, were set upon by demolition workers in the middle of one June night in 1970, despite the fact that they had been occupied by students and preservationists intent on keeping them intact. And similar efforts to preserve a house on Ely Place, once the home of Oliver St John Gogarty, and Frascati House in Blackrock, former residence of Lord Edward FitzGerald, about the same time met with similar fates. It was as if nothing had been learned from the wanton destruction of so much of the city's heritage during the 1960s.

In the early 1970s, however, what many people thought Ireland and Dublin needed was the strong leadership of a figure who would have an interest not just in politics but in the arts and heritage. In the area of the arts the administration of Taoiseach Charles Haughey was not only progressive but innovative, improving conditions for writers and artists with the introduction of tax-free status for royalty earnings, and with the establishment in 1981 of Aosdána, the self-regulating academy of letters and fine arts.

THE LATE 1970S

The mid and late 1970s saw further significant improvements in the art and arts-related world in Dublin. The Chester Beatty Library, a world-renowned collection of oriental art and manuscripts held in a purpose-built library in Ballsbridge, and willed to the state by Sir Alfred Chester Beatty, was opened by President Cearbhall Ó Dálaigh in July 1975 (and would in 1999 be moved to larger premises in Dublin Castle). The opening of the Project Arts Centre in Dublin's still under-developed Temple Bar gave a much needed boost to the arts in the south city, similar to what the Grapevine Arts Centre would provide in the North.

Population is an obvious indicator of growth but other

kinds of indicators also exist. The continued growth of Dublin throughout this period, for instance, can be seen in the 1976 decision to publish, for the first time, two separate Irish telephone directories, one for Dublin and one for the rest of the country. It was as if there was now, in almost every house in the land, a reminder of the extraordinary and continuing growth of the city in which one third of the population of the Republic, and almost one quarter of the population of the entire island, now lived.

Whatever about communications within the city and country, however, communications between Ireland and the outside world took a downward turn in July 1976 with the assassination in Sandyford, County Dublin, of the British Ambassador, Christopher Ewart-Biggs, just weeks after he had presented his credentials to the President. The assassination once again raised uncomfortable questions about the support base of the IRA within the Republic, and provoked a joint declaration from the Dáil and Seanad (the upper house) that 'a national emergency exists affecting the vital interests of the state'. The following decades of murders, retaliations and massacres, notably in Northern Ireland, would show that an emergency can be a very long time in Irish politics. Indeed, an historic attempt to sail to America, just months before the Ewart-Biggs assassination, in a reconstruction of the leather *curragh* supposed to have carried St Brendan across the Atlantic some 1,500 years before, might unkindly be seen as further proof that, in many respects, the Ireland of the period was more comfortable with revisiting the glories of its past than dealing with the reality of its present.

In Dublin, meanwhile, controversial planning policies were again making the news with the occupation by more than seventy students of premises on Pembroke Street designated for development as the headquarters of Bord na Móna, the peat fuel board. The completion, also in 1978, of Sam Stephenson's cube-shaped Central Bank on Dame Street (the first and so far only building in Dublin to have its floors suspended from the roof by visible structural cables) aroused strong feelings on both sides in the debate about the rapidly changing face of Dublin and the direction to be taken when modernising streets of a predominantly Georgian character.

The strikes of the period – so common now that the occasional absence of demonstrators on Dublin streets was almost more remarkable than their presence – included, in February 1979, for the first time in half a century, a five-month stoppage by postal workers. The overlapping strike by bin collectors almost brought the city to a halt. The same confused period saw a number of anti-nuclear demonstrations against government plans to build a nuclear power plant in the south-east of the country (though it took large-scale demonstrations on the site of the proposed station itself at Carnsore, County Wexford before the government abandoned its plans).

18

THE SHOPPING CENTRE: DUBLIN IN THE 1980S AND 1990S

Among the many plans to revitalise the centre of Dublin as it entered the 1980s was the attempt to introduce European-style shopping centres, a move which has transformed not only the look of the city but the manner in which it functions commercially. Markets, which had survived for generations in areas like Moore Street in the city centre were now to be replaced, or severely limited and regulated, by some of the largest secular buildings erected in the city's history. In 1981 alone, two of the first of many large shopping complexes opened, the ILAC Centre in Henry Street on the north side (in a clever move creating a home for the main Dublin City Library), and the refurbished Powerscourt House in South William Street, a tasteful refurbishment of the great house with interior courtyard, and generally greeted with enthusiasm by Dubliners who might have been forgiven for imagining that all such developments were destructive by their very nature. Indeed, the Powerscourt complex, along with the pedestrianisation of Grafton Street only yards away, has helped to give the south city centre its distinctive laid-back yet upmarket feel, a feat never quiet equalled on the north side, despite the pedestrianisation of Henry and North Earl streets on opposite sides of O'Connell Street.

Many of the difficulties of the north inner city can be traced to the decline of O'Connell Street itself, blighted first by an influx of fast-food emporia and gaudy neon signs, and then by the closure and decline of the area around the Carlton cinema for the building of a city centre conference centre which never materialised. (Early 1999, however, would see the unveiling of plans completely to redevelop this site and surrounding properties, along with neighbouring backstreets right down to the ILAC Centre, as yet another new shopping hub expected to revitalise the area.)

If the appearance of cathedral-like shopping centres was a major feature of the Dublin of this period, commercial premises were not the only ones undergoing something of a revolution. The wonderful reinvention of the Royal Hospital Kilmainham (for years little more than a storeroom for broken-down statuary) as the Irish Museum of Modern Art (IMMA) in 1985 continued an upward trend begun with the re-opening of the old University College building on Earlsfort Terrace, off St Stephen's Green, as the sumptuous National Concert Hall in 1981.

(An interesting aside concerns the Richmond Tower gate at the western entrance to the Royal Hospital grounds. The building in 1844 of nearby Kingsbridge Station in what was then described, intriguingly, as 'a field . . . in the county of the city of Dublin' marked the beginning of a major change in travel and traffic patterns in Dublin and in particular on its quays. One sign of this change was the taking apart, brick by brick, and the rebuilding in its present location of Richmond Tower which had up to then stood at the foot of Watling Street as the entrance to Watling Bridge. The arrival of the railway, it seems, created a commuter traffic which, even in the mid-nineteenth century, required more and more space. Developments such as the opening in 1982 of an auxiliary bridge to deal with the heavy traffic around Heuston Station showed that the problem of congestion in the area was far from solved.)

Throughout the mid 1980s, the traffic problem continued to escalate, despite the quality bus corridors (QBCs) that had been opened on routes across the city since the beginning of the decade. Allied to traffic congestion was the steadily deteriorating quality of city air, recognised in an 1982 EC survey which declared Dublin the most air-polluted capital in the entire European Community. The phasing out of bituminous coal, like the coming on-stream of natural gas in 1984 and the introduction of lead-free motoring fuels, went some small way towards helping clear the air and encourage both habitation and leisure in the city as it entered the final decade of the twentieth century. But the real problem was the sheer number of cars on streets designed for pedestrians and horses.

The completion of the Dublin Area Rapid Transit electric train system (DART), begun in 1980, and running from Howth to Bray, was within months of its opening in 1984 a major success in the fight against congestion, and immediately led to discussions about the possibilities of similar lines to Tallaght and points west. It also led to the inevitable round of debate about the feasibility of the reopening of the Harcourt Street line which, although it too had terminated in Bray, had *en route* served bustling non-coastal suburbs such as Ranelagh and Dundrum. But the financial boom that was at once to swell the price and the demand for real estate through the 1990s (a boom made possible, partly, by clever use of European subventions and structural funds) would do little to alleviate the city's now critical traffic congestion.

TEMPLE BAR

Depending on one's standpoint, Temple Bar is either one of the great successes or one of the great failures of vision in the recent history of Dublin. Nowadays the name Temple Bar instantly suggests a small nexus of streets lined with loud bars, fashionable restaurants and art-related spaces (a kind of cross between the Left Bank in Paris and a Majorcan holiday resort). This is truly extraordinary when one considers just how run-down most of the buildings were until the early 1990s.

Run-down, yes, but not vacant. For what happened in Temple Bar between the 1950s, when the decay began in earnest, and the present when it is arguably the most sought-after and fashionable real estate in Ireland, is a tale of life in the city returning almost to the very spot where it first began, in and around the south bank of the Liffey. And what is truly extraordinary about that economic and social rebirth, whether for good or bad, is that it was artists and musicians in the main who led the way.

The earliest record of the existence of Temple Bar dates from a late seventeeth-century map featuring a 'bar', or sandbank walkway, in the area of Wellington Quay. Named for Sir William Temple, Provost of Trinity College, whose lands bordered the river (and in imitation of a Temple Bar already then in existence in London), the area's main claim to fame from the 1950s until the late 1980s was that it was run-down, occasionally dangerous, and believed by many to be on its way to becoming a new Monto for the south side.

What actually happened was very different. From 1981 onwards, whole blocks of the area between Westmoreland and Parliament streets were bought up by CIE (then the national bus and rail company) with the intention of building a central Dublin bus depot there. When the depot plan was shelved – the additional traffic would have made a difficult situation intolerable – the run-down buildings were rented and leased to artists as studios, semi-private galleries and occasionally as residences. With such 'character' firmly established in the area at abnormally low rents, and with real estate right across the city rising dramatically in value through the 1980s, it was only a matter of time before business concerns took notice.

Temple Bar Properties, a government-established company, was set up in 1991 to 'oversee the development of the Temple Bar area and the creation of Dublin's Cultural Quarter', though many argue that the area, which was by then already something of a cultural quarter, is today dominated by loud, quick-turnover bars and clubs, and that the alternative art and music scenes which were the area's real attraction are now all but marginalised. On the other hand, there can be no doubt that the commercial success of Temple Bar and Temple Bar Properties has helped in the revitalisation of the city centre in general, and it may be just a matter of time before this still very young experiment finds that elusive but critical balance between commercial and leisure activities.

INTO THE NINETIES

The 1980s and early 1990s saw Dublin transformed beyond the wildest dreams of Pearse, Larkin or Grattan. The biggest crowds seen in the city in those years were not revolutionaries or demonstrators but members of the congregation at Pope John Paul II's mass in the Phoenix Park in September 1979 (over one million), and just over ten years later approximately half that number when fans packed the streets to welcome home from *Italia '90* the defeated Republic of Ireland World Cup soccer team.

Dublin is, of course, a city without a planned central square or plaza sufficient to contain such large gatherings (a fact evidently overlooked by the Wide Streets Commission). Aggregations on a grand scale, therefore, tend to take place either in the Phoenix Park or in the limited space at College Green, between the Bank of Ireland and the front gates of Trinity College, crowds backing up into the streets all around. College Green, of course, was originally Hoggen Green (*hogges* meaning mound), a raised place in the centre of the original Viking settlement where executions, speeches and meetings of all kinds might take place. As the city grew and changed shape drastically, somehow something of the purpose of this area has managed to survive, and in large gatherings there is something of a sense of continuum to be found here, a sense sometimes equalled in Christ Church Place when crowds gather on the last night of December to ring in the New Year.

An interesting echo of modern day mass gatherings in College Green is to be found in a short extract from Charles Maturin's 1818 novel entitled *Women* in which a crowd gathers on hearing the news that allied troops have finally managed to enter Paris.

> The whole population of Dublin appeared concentrated in College Green, – carriages stopping by dozens before the placards, – horsemen rising on tiptoe in their stirrups above the heads of the crowd, to read them – and the crowd, wedged head to head, and foot to foot, planted by hundreds and by thousands, gazing, devouring with mouths, eyes, and ears all that could be heard, seen or swallowed.

Certainly anyone who has attended one of the fireworks or other spectacles connected with, for example, the St Patrick's Day festivals of recent years, will recognise the scene.

That religion or politics are no longer the only attractions for crowds of such size says much about changes in life in the city; that the people of the country as a whole have, in less than a generation, taken what many regarded as detested foreign games so much to their hearts says even more about changing attitudes to what constitutes Irishness and how that nebulous entity might be defined. The appearance on the pitch of international star Pele at Dalymount Park in 1972, when Santos beat Bohemians, was a key moment in the extraordinary sequence of events which has made soccer a serious contender with Gaelic football and hurling as the most popular national sport. Indeed, many feel that it cannot be long before the Gaelic Athletic Association (GAA) agree to lift their ban on the playing of the game in their state-of-the-art stadium at Croke Park.

Article 44.1 of the Irish Constitution held that the Catholic Church was 'the guardian of the Faith professed by the great majority of the citizens' but that clause was quietly dropped in 1973 and, in recent years, that great majority has both significantly fallen in numbers and, at the same time, has had to learn to accommodate the views and beliefs of citizens of many different religious per suasions. The economic boom of the 1990s, with its so-called 'Celtic Tiger' economy, has made Ireland, perhaps for the first time ever, a destination for those seeking employment. Less happily, since the late 1970s, there has been a steady stream of refugees and asylum seekers seeking to build new lives for themselves in the city. This stream began with the Vietnamese boat people of the late 1970s, continued as many middle European nationals, following the collapse of Communism, sought a haven here, and was again swelled first by the Bosnian refugees of the early 1990s and later in the decade by those fleeing what is now called 'ethnic cleansing' in other former Yugoslav republics.

The horrors of these wars, of course, is out of all scale with anything seen in Ireland over its bloody history. But what Ireland, and Dublin in particular, can learn from their survivors is the importance of tolerance and appreciation of difference formerly inapplicable in this monocultural society. Whereas the slackening of influence of the Catholic Church is, at least chronologically, associated with the advent of television and the other mass media, it is somewhat ironic that the advent of a diverse and pluralist society was marked by one of its most ardent opponents, Archbishop John Charles McQuaid, to whom fell the duty of performing the opening blessing ceremony of the new national television service back in 1961.

This is not, of course, to say that the Catholic Church has embraced the many changes in Irish and Dublin society in the second half of the twentieth century. Certainly revelations about the horrific abuse of children in many religious institutions throughout the country have forced change, and accountability, where that change was formerly resisted. In Dublin, where some of the worst revelations concerned national institutions such as laundries run by the Sisters of Mercy at Islandbridge and the home of the Artane Boys Band (which for generations has played at every All-Ireland Football and Hurling Final at Croke Park, like some symbol of all that is good and changeless about the country), the shock was deeply felt and the effect is as yet difficult to gauge. Certainly it is likely to result in a continued falling away from organised religion, a falling away that has been happening, gradually, over the last couple of generations.

In this and other respects, Dublin has certainly

changed, perhaps even 'changed utterly', as Yeats had it in another context. For the city is now one of the commercial success stories of Europe, and one of its most popular and fashionable destinations (with visitors regularly outnumbering inhabitants in recent years, by as much as 3:1 according to some sources). The renovation of the Temple Bar area and the revitalisation of the inner city with new apartment complexes, facilitated to a great extent by EU urban renewal and tax relief schemes, have caused parts of the city to become almost unrecognisable in little more than a decade. The appearance of massive shopping complexes in Tallaght, Blanchardstown and other suburban areas from the mid 1990s onwards has challenged the dominance of city-centre stores and arguably led to more choice for at least those consumers with access to cars. Certainly the fears that many voters had about Ireland's entry into first the European Economic Community (in 1972), then the European Monetary System, and, most recently, its signing up for the Single European Currency appear to have been unfounded.

There is, of course, a dark side. In Dublin in particular, new residential and shopping developments aside, the 1980s and 1990s are as likely to be remembered for the massive heroin problem which began in the inner city and spread outwards when left unchallenged. This was a problem which was swept under the political carpet. Indeed the activities of so-called 'drug barons' present one of the greatest challenges to society since the founding of the state, though new agencies such as the Criminal Assets Bureau (CAB), established after the murder of journalist Veronica Guerin in 1997 and given the power to confiscate the goods and property of suspected drugs criminals, are finally beginning to make an impact.

Other factors which have had considerable influence on change in the last decade of the twentieth century include the presidency of Mary Robinson, who served from the beginning of the decade until 1997. Robinson was perhaps the most socially influential president in the history of the state, not only because she was the country's first woman president (succeeded by another woman, Mary McAleese), but because she was proactive, a president who made it her business to connect with women's groups and community groups throughout the city and country, and particularly with those battling the twin, and often connected scourges of high unemployment and drug addiction. Her widespread support from the majority of the country's population seems extraordinary given the disapproval she attracted back in 1971 when, as a young lawyer, she attempted to introduce a bill in the Seanad regarding the liberalisation of the law governing the availability of contraceptives. (In a typically Irish fudge, at the time their sale, but not their use, was prohibited. It was Charles Haughey, then the Minister for Health, who in 1979 introduced a bill which legalised the sale of condoms, though distribution was to be strictly limited to married couples on production of a doctor's prescription.)

YOUTH CULTURE

When it comes to examining the phenomenal popularity of Dublin as a tourist attraction (for everyone from quiet backpackers to larger groups celebrating impending weddings and all categories in between), the 1980s and 1990s force social analysts to consider the importance of a subject not usually in their remit: that of youth culture, and in particular of popular music. The rise to dominance of rock supergroup U2 through these two decades not only helped clear the way and prepare a world audience for other Irish bands and artists, but for the first time showed that music was a major contributor to the country's GNP and was therefore, just as film would be recognised to be, deserving of investment and subvention. Even bands and individuals who had been ambassadors of Irish music for decades before U2 seemed to be reborn in the wave of popularity for all things Irish.

One phenomenon which both aroused massive debate and contributed to a new cultural stereotype of Dublin as a microcosm of the Wild West was the adoption of what was once the thriving horse culture of the city by the young people of outlying estates such as Clondalkin and Finglas. That this culture seemed to have been born out of a forced juxtaposition of members of the settled and travelling communities on such estates is perhaps the most remarkable aspect of the phenomenon. According to critic Fintan O'Toole, in the introduction to *Pony Kids,* a book of photographs by Perry Ogden, 'One of the simplest explanations of the pony kid culture is the easy availability of cheap horses.' At the same time O'Toole was at pains to point out the reasons why the culture had taken such a hold in the first place. 'Keeping horses enriches the lives of these kids,' he wrote, 'helps them to develop a sense of responsibility, and diverts them from destructive alternatives.' Though those destructive alternatives had often included the stealing and driving at speed of stolen cars, what worried many people was the by-now-frequent sight of maltreated and untended horses in some traffic-heavy areas. A further, if small-scale concern was occasioned by the adoption of the pony as a convenient means of transport between outlying estates by a number of enterprising heroin dealers. Irish cinema's worship of the sight of piebald ponies passing burnt-out cars and kids with skipping ropes was just one aspect of a more complicated story.

In the end, the Control of Horses Act introduced in 1997 probably signalled the beginning of the demise of the pony culture of the Dublin suburbs, though the Smithfield Market in the north city centre continues to take place every month, attracting large numbers of buyers and sellers and perhaps even larger numbers of spectators intrigued by this glimpse into a hidden Dublin with echoes of a horse-dependent past.

Also interesting, though perhaps coincidental, is the fact that in 1998 mounted police returned to the streets of Dublin after an absence of seventy-nine years. The Garda Mounted Unit, formed in May of that year, consists of six horses, for the moment covering the wider city centre area. Allied to the obvious advantages of horses in controlling crowds, the official Garda website further suggested that 'Horses are also a warm attraction for people, helping to break down barriers and providing a calming effect.'

18

The Future of Dublin

With the current pace of development, the next fifty or hundred years may well bring changes in Dublin as dramatic as those experienced in the previous thousand. For one thing the city is now growing at such a pace that bordering towns such as Balbriggan to the north, Lucan and Naas to the west and Bray to the south will very soon be part of the greater metropolitan area. By then, perhaps as much as half of the country's entire population will call themselves Dubliners, as the word comes to denote the citizens of an ever larger geographical area.

With all the changes and expansion, all the financial improvements and plans to break the traffic deadlock (underground tunnels and overground light rail systems having been first proposed as far back as the early 1970s), few things other than the presence and direction of the river Liffey remain constant.

First called Anna Livia when her Irish name *Abha na Life* became Latinised in the middle of the nineteenth century, the Liffey was subsequently transformed into the goddess-like figure of Anna Livia Plurabelle in Joyce's *Finnegans Wake*. Though much narrower now than when the Vikings first glimpsed her and, certainly in her city stretches, less graced by trout and other freshwater fish, little about her has really changed. While other Dublin rivers and streams (more than fifty of them in all) have gone underground over the years, the Liffey still rises near the Sally Gap in County Wicklow, flows more or less northwards towards the plain of Dublin, then greets the city as it passes with 'Soft morning, city! Lsp! I am leafy speafing', as Joyce transcribed her whisperings, and makes her way inexorably to the sea.

Some things seem never to change. Though just over two hundred years old the two canals seem somehow ageless. Near the northern one, just like Brendan Behan a generation before them, young offenders listen from their Mountjoy prison cells as

The auld triangle goes jingle-jangle
All along the banks of the Royal Canal,

though nowadays the 'auld triangle' of passing barges is more likely to be the blare of traffic horns or the rhythmic sweep of the Garda observation helicopter, an almost nightly sight hovering over the city's crime blackspots.

Whether staying put or returning from abroad, however, joining the thousands of families in the ever-expanding suburbs or, for the first time in a century, opting to live in its thriving, bustling centre, the citizens of Dublin, now a city of many colours, races and creeds, must work together to ensure that these same ancient and more recent bodies of water reflect a new maturity, among city planners, politicians and citizens alike in years to come.

BIBLIOGRAPHY

Bennett, D. *Encyclopedia of Dublin*. Gill and Macmillan, 1991.

Bradley, J. ed. *Viking Dublin Exposed*. O'Brien Press, 1984.

Caprani, V. *A Walk around Dublin*. Appletree Press, 1992.

Clarke, H. B. ed. *Medieval Dublin: The Living City*. Irish Academic Press, 1990.

Conlin, S. *Historic Dublin*. O'Brien Press, 1986.

Craig, M. *Dublin 1660–1860*. Allen Figgis Ltd., 1980.

Crealey, A. *An Irish Almanac*. Mercier Press, 1993.

de Courcey, J. *Anna Liffey: The River of Dublin*. O'Brien Press, 1988.

Ferguson, P. *A-Z of Georgian Dublin*. Harry Margary, 1998.

Foster, R. F. *Modern Ireland 1600–1972*. Allen Lane, 1988.

Gilespie, E. ed. *The Liberties of Dublin*. O'Brien Press, 1973.

Guinness, D. *Portrait of Dublin*. Batsford, 1967.

Healy, E. *The Wolfhound Guide to Dublin Monuments*. Wolfhound Press, 1998.

Igoe, V. *Literary Guide to Dublin*. Methuen, 1995.

Johnston, M. *Around the Banks of Pimlico*. Attic Press, 1985.

Kearns, K. C. *Dublin Tenement Life: An Oral History*. Gill and Macmillan, 1994.

Lalor, B. *Dublin*. Routledge and Kegan Paul, 1981.

Lalor, B. *The Ultimate Dublin Guide*. O'Brien Press, 1991.

Lehane, B. *Dublin*. The Great Cities, Time-Life Books, 1978.

Liddy, P. *Dublin Today. Irish Times,* 1984.

Liddy, P. *Walking Dublin.* New Holland Publishers, 1998.

Lydon, J. *The Making of Ireland.* Routledge, 1998.

MacLoughlin, A. *Guide to Historic Dublin.* Gill and Macmillan, 1979.

Moody, T. W., F. X. Martin and F. J., Byrne eds. *A New History of Ireland.* Clarendon Press, 1976-87.

O'Brien, J, and D. Guinness. *Dublin: A Grand Tour.* Weidenfeld, 1994.

O'Donnel, E. E. *The Annals of Dublin: Fair City.* Wolfhound Press, 1987.

Prunty, J. *Dublin Slums, 1800–1925.* Irish Academic Press, 1998.

Redmond, B. *The Story of Dublin City and County.* Browne and Nolan Ltd., 1927.

Somerville-Large, P. *Irish Eccentrics.* Hamish Hamilton, 1975.

Sweeney, C. L. *Rivers of Dublin.* Dublin Corporation, 1991.

INDEX

British Army, 103
British Commonwealth, 48
British Empire, 113
Bronze Age, 10
Browne, Archbishop George, 37
Bruce, Edward, 28-9
Bruce, Robert, 28-9
Brugha, Cathal, 104
Bull Wall, 73
Burke, Thomas H., 89
Butler, James *see* Earl of Ormond and Ossory
Butler, Máire, 102
Butlers, Earls of Ormond, 32, 45
Butt, Isaac, 86-8

Cairo Gang, 103
Capel Street Bridge, 52
Carew, George, 41
Carlisle Bridge (later O'Connell Bridge), 66, 67
Carnslore, County Wexford, 130
Carson, Edward, 102
Casement, Roger, 97, 99
Cassels, 60
Castle Street, 44
Catherine of Aragon, 35, 39
Catholic Association, 74
Catholic Emancipation, 73-4, 75
Catholic University, 82
Cavendish, Lord Frederick, 89
Celtic Tiger economy, 138
Celts, the, 10, 12
censorship, 113-4
    Censorship of Publications Act amended, 121-2
Central Bank, 130
Charles I, King, 43, 46
    execution of, 48
Charles II, King, 50, 52
    Restoration, 51
charter, first and second to Dublin, by Henry II, 24-5
charter, third, by Prince John, 25

Chester Beatty Library, 128
Chester Beatty, Sir Alfred, 128
Childers, Erskine, 96
Chrish Church Place, 137
Christ Church Cathedral, 16, 21, 33, 90
Christianisation of Dublin, 12-13
Church of Ireland, 40, 51, 59, 60
Churchill, Winston, 111-2
civil rights movement, 126
Civil War, 105, 106, 107
    killing of Kevin O'Higgins, 109-10
Clarke, Tom, 97, 101
Clement II, Pope, 26
Clerkenwell jail, 85
Clontarf (suburb), 84
Clontarf rally (O'Connell), 76-7
Clontarf, Battle of, 21
College Green, 56, 136-7
Collins, Michael, 101, 102-5
    killed in Civil War, 105
Common Council, 75
Confederation of Kilkenny, 45- 7
Conn of the Hundred Battles, King, 14, 17
Connolly, James, 86, 94, 95, 99, 101
Conservative Party, 89
Control of Horses Act, 143
Cook Street, 41
Coombe, the, 26
    immigration of French Huguenot refugees, 54
Corn Laws, 79
Cornmarket, 16
Cosgrave, William T., 105
Costello, John A., 112
Counter-Reformation, 38, 41
Crime and Outrage Act, 77
Criminal Assets Bureau (CAB), 140
Croke Park, 103, 138, 139
Cromwell, Henry, 49-50